DIRECT RED

Gabriel Weston

Direct Red

A Surgeon's View of Her Life-or-Death Profession

BOND
STREET
BOOKS

DOUBLEDAY
CANADA

Doubleday Canada and colophon are trademarks

Library and Archives Canada Cataloguing in Publication

Weston, Gabriel
Direct red : a surgeon's story / Gabriel Weston.

ISBN 978-0-385-66580-3

1. Weston, Gabriel. 2. Surgeons--Great Britain--Biography.
3. Hospital care--Great Britain. I. Title.

RD27.35.W44A3 2009   617.092   C2008-906912-9

Typeset in AjenMM by Palimpsest Book Production Limited,
Grangemouth, Stirlingshire

Printed and bound in the USA

Published in Canada by Bond Street Books,
a division of Random House of Canada Limited

Visit Random House of Canada Limited's website: www.randomhouse.ca

10   9   8   7   6   5   4   3   2   1

To Ander

AUTHOR'S NOTE

This book is not literally true. While its characters owe something to patients and doctors I have known, none of these characters is real. Similarly, events I describe are a mixture of things that have happened and things that might have happened.

G.W.

CONTENTS

1. Speed   1

2. Sex   10

3. Death   24

4. Voices   36

5. Beauty   52

6. Hierarchy   65

7. Territory   81

8. Emergencies   91

9. Ambition   103

10. Help   114

11. Children   134

12. Appearances   151

13. Changes   161

14. Home   172

    Acknowledgements   183

SPEED

I am about to faint. *Methylene Blue. Acridine Orange.* I have been holding someone's neck open for seven hours. During this time, my consultant has asked me the same four anatomy questions he asks me every week, but otherwise there has been no conversation. Heart 106.2 is on the third loop of its same old songs. *Saffron. Malachite Green.* My back is cold with sweat under a synthetic, unsoakable surgical gown. My mask feels suffocating, its visor as dirty as a windscreen, spattered with today's roadkill. I am beginning to feel queasily insubstantial and the continuity of my vision is breaking up. *Tyrian Purple. Hoffman's Violet.* And just as I am about to confess my shame and excuse myself from the table, my mantra begins to work. *Direct Red.* The open wound in front of me seems to reconfigure. I start hearing sounds normally again. I stop feeling sick. No one has noticed.

What to do when you feel unwell in theatre is never discussed, but it is my private belief that all surgeons have these moments of incapacity, and that we each try to save ourselves differently. At medical school, while studying pathology, I was charmed by the names of the colourful dyes used to stain tissues for clearer microscopic viewing. Crystalline as jewels, primary as food colourings used for cake icing and egg painting, the names of these elixirs seemed brighter in my mind than the substances themselves, the Platonic hues offset by their arcane prefixes. And through a process I cannot chart, every time I feel sick in theatre, I summon a rainbow collage of these names to mind. They stimulate my ebbing consciousness and usually call me back from that strange physiological precipice to normal function.

For me, such moments of near collapse are heralded not by dearth of sleep, excess of alcohol, or lack of breakfast. I never stay up late or drink on the eve of surgery; I am always ravenous in anticipation of it. No, it is *long* operations I cannot tolerate, slowness which gets the better of me, lack of pace which makes me ill. This personal feeling chimes with a more openly acknowledged association I have observed throughout my surgical career between speed and competence on the one hand, slowness and ineptitude on the other.

Slowness characterised the worst surgery I have witnessed. It was my first night ever on call as a general surgery junior. Arriving as a clinical virgin to this daunting duty, I learned that my registrar was suffering from pneumonia and had just been given a bed on one of the medical wards. I would be without clinical supervision in the hospital for the entire shift and should call my consultant at home if I needed any help.

In the middle of the night, the emergency voice facility on my bleep summoned me down to casualty: 'Trauma call! General surgeon to A&E! Please go straight to A&E Resus!' As I ran down the three flights of stairs and the long corridor towards my fate, all I could think at this threshold of my training was 'There's not a single situation that I will know how to handle', feeling keenly the lack of a senior doctor there to guide me.

Surprisingly, the scenario that greeted me was so clear that I did know what to do. My patient was a young woman who had been shot in the abdomen in a local nightclub. She had a hole in her belly where the bullet had entered and no obvious exit wound. Her whole trunk was growing in size before my eyes and was tense to the touch, a sure sign of serious intra-abdominal bleeding. I knew that this woman needed to go immediately to theatre to be opened up and that no investigations or messing about should delay her journey. I felt relieved the decision was such an easy one and asked the A&E staff to get her ready for surgery. I then phoned the on-call consultant, offering to meet him in theatre. 'Not so fast,' he objected. 'You youngsters are always in such a hurry.'

It was the first halt in a night which was characterised by this consultant's appalling reluctance to act fast. When I return to it in my mind, the whole course of events plays itself out to me in slow motion, as if underwater. My foolish boss took half an hour to turn up. He appeared in casualty with his hands in his pockets and wasted time showing off his knowledge of firearms to the attendant policemen. He ridiculed my sense of urgency. He recommended an unnecessary scan when it was plain to see that a young woman was dying in front of him and desperately needed an operation. When he finally did concede that we needed to go to theatre, he picked up an instant coffee on the way.

Fortunately, physiology forced pace on a situation which otherwise seemed inexorably slow: once we cut the woman open from breastbone to pubis and cleared her gut out of the way with one deep sweep, we were confronted with the sight of the enormous hollow cavern of the patient's abdomen filling with blood as quickly as a basin fills with water. The two large suction drains given me by the nurse could not keep up with the loss and blood tipped over the sides, onto us, onto the floor. Later that morning, when I removed my surgical scrubs in the empty gloaming of the women's changing room, my underwear was wet with this woman's blood and I remember thinking bizarrely and grandiosely of myself like Macbeth and how I too might 'the multitudinous seas incarnadine' after such a night.

When I look back now, it seems implausible that this consultant did not have a clue what to do, that he didn't know the simplest emergency measures of clamping the aorta or even packing the abdomen with swabs to buy some time. He dressed his incompetence in a mannered slowness of action, and this made his thinking fatally sluggish. It took him almost an hour to admit he wasn't coping, at which point he became desperate and was shouting at the scrub nurse, 'Get me another surgeon! Any surgeon!' Another hour passed before the regional vascular consultant was able to reach the hospital to sort things out. For this patient, it was too late, and though she survived the night after the second surgeon managed to find and repair the holes in her iliac vessels, she died the following day from multiple organ failure, probably as a result of massive blood loss.

This horrible scenario has never left me. Although I was far too junior at that time for any sensible suggestions to have been expected of me, the night taught me the paramount value of a quick response.

And in fact, many of my most talented cutting teachers have been fast. One brilliant general surgeon was speed personified. It was almost impossible to keep up with him on ward rounds; his operations were performed as if revved up. He would dissect right down on top of dangerous vessels, explaining, 'Know your enemy.' As I closed his wounds, my neophyte hands trembling awkwardly with the needle-holder, he would stand behind me, commanding, 'Quick! Quick! Like a Singer sewing machine!'

Another surgeon I know, also highly esteemed, encapsulates the same association. Not only impressively quick with his hands, his hobby is motocross bike racing; his reputation and strength are inextricably linked to alacrity.

Indeed, the very idiom of surgery accords a thrilling significance to those things we do quickly. Cardiothoracic surgeons 'crack the chest' when they need emergency access to it, transplant surgeons 'snatch' kidneys for donation. In ENT, swift access to the airway in dire straits is gained with the knife by a 'slash trachy'. We love to curl these terms round our tongues, and such speedy actions are the ones we long to perform.

All these factors were at play this week when I made my terrible mistake – an aversion to slowness, keenness to be quick, the presence of an impatient, talented boss.

Since meeting The Lion, I have been afflicted by a more than routine respect. My boss is known for many things, his stinging irascibility, his prodigious surgical skill, his vast humour. My desire to impress is that of the suitor for the object of their affection, the groundling for the idol. When he addresses me, I feel like light is shining on me; he calls me his 'desperate housewife' and I feel special.

In theatre on that fateful day, I find myself prepared to excise submandibular glands in two consecutive patients, a rare opportunity indeed to follow one lesson immediately with its image. I have done my reading the night before surgery and am academically ready for the challenge. On several occasions, I have seen The Lion complete this operation in under twenty minutes. This is my first ever, though, and I am a slow operator. With my esteemed boss behind me, I begin: skin incision, haemostasis, raising the capsule to avoid damage to an important branch of the facial nerve. Already half an hour has gone. The Lion is behind me shifting from foot to foot. I feel his very physical proximity which no other situation would allow and, with it, the full weight of his fond expectation. 'Take your time,' he says repeatedly, his tone belying his words.

Thirty minutes later, I have found and tied off the facial vessels. All that remains is to ligate the salivary duct and release the gland from its bed. Knowing the operation is drawing to a close and in a display that is more humorous than threatening, my boss walks to the door which leads from the operating theatre. Mockingly, he says, 'I'm getting bored now, Doctor. I'm going to leave the room unless I see some action.' I know that most of this is fun, but also feel I am being measured specifically by my pace. I start to cut the remaining tissue rather more quickly than is comfortable. I don't want to be left unsupervised and, more importantly, cannot bear the idea that I may be destined to join the ranks of the incompetent dawdlers. I finish up; the operation has taken over an hour.

By the time I write my operation note, the next submandibular gland is etherised upon the table. I am determined to prove myself this time. With the last gland preserved fresh in my mind, I see no reason why I should not act with little guidance and finish up more quickly than before. I want to restore The Lion's faith in me.

I approach the table, prep and drape the patient, mark out my intended incision two fingerbreadths below the line of the jaw in order to preserve the marginal mandibular nerve, and infiltrate sparkling local anaesthetic from a small syringe. A necessary hiatus of two minutes while this takes effect gives me pause to plan and I gather my wits. The Lion has taken up his position behind me and he is still again, as if in hope. I declare my intentions to him with my first cut which is fast, firm and unfussy. One further stroke and – to my pleasure – the enlarged submandibular gland peeps through its capsule, glassy as an eyeball. I penetrate this confining layer without difficulty, allowing the gland to offer itself to me. No one has spoken; my boss has made no quips, ventured no prods in the back. I feel glad and full of purpose, like a boat whose sail has caught the wind.

Unfortunately, my grace ends as I attempt to mobilise the gland. Every cut seems to prompt bleeding. My view is clouded by ooze. My progress has become slow and stolid. 'Sialadenitis,' my consultant mutters, and in declaring that this salivary gland has been chronically scarred by inflammation, he seems to be forgiving me my loss of tempo. Grindingly and anxiously, I proceed. I tie off several vessels which enter the gland and am not absolutely sure which of them are the facial artery and vein, so distorted is the geography by years of disease. The Lion doesn't hound me but walks away and approaches the table by turns, punctuating his laborious attendance with small chats with the various theatre staff. I feel a heavy disappointment at having all but lost his attention. A couple of the neighbouring operating lists have finished and quite a crowd has gathered in theatre now, the main attraction not me but my charismatic boss and his management of a rookie.

The operation is now nearly over and, as before, nearly an hour has passed. I have tied off Wharton's duct and the gland is hanging from a pedicle which I am carefully dissecting with clips. Impatient now – both in truth and for show – and keen to display mastery, The Lion goads, 'Cut it, come on.' I demur, no longer trying to win any races and wanting to relish my last moments of agency. Louder now, he repeats, 'Cut it! What are you, chicken? Cut it, chicken!' I can't resist, appose thumb to hand within my scissors and a second later blood sprays a foot across the room. I have cut the facial artery, hiding within that last stalk of unsevered tissue. The spectators move perceptibly forward a little, now glad to have chosen this theatre, this show. I try to find the end of the artery to stem its pulsing flow but soon capitulate and ask for help. I feel slow, clumsy, dangerous and ashamed. The Lion steps forward and with a deftness that shows me the extent of my own lack of skill, he identifies and ties off the culprit artery in less than a minute. The patient is safe again.

Later, when the mess and company are cleared, The Lion approaches me and gently ventures, 'I ruined that for you.' This is his apology and I accept it with mock bravura, 'No. You didn't. Just don't call me chicken again!'

Looking back on this incident now from an operating table I have been standing at all day, I feel the absurdity and hubris of my seduction by speed. I do not yet know whether I will make a good surgeon, but the fact that I am slow at the moment doesn't in itself make me a bad one. My boss is carefully sewing up. The day is nearly over.

SEX

To be a good doctor, you have to master a paradoxical art. You need to get close to a patient so that they will tell you things and you will understand what they mean. But you also have to keep distant enough not to get too affected. This distance keeps both parties safe. A doctor can't afford to faint at the sight of blood or retch on smelling faeces. And the last thing a person wants when they have been told awful news is for their doctor to start crying. But sometimes, you feel the likeness between you and your patient more than the difference. Sometimes, your own body declares its fallibility as if in sympathy for the person you are consulting, or your heart defies you by responding just when you least want it to. One of the most difficult things is learning how to manage sexual matters in hospital life. It's like going through adolescence all over again.

The first time I ever touched a stranger's penis, I was lucky enough that it was a patient under general anaesthetic. The old man, who had been wheeled unconscious into the operating theatre from the anaesthetic room, was due for a left hemicolectomy for cancer, a long operation which requires a urinary catheter for monitoring.

I was a house officer. I knew I loved being in theatre but as yet had no useful place in it. I was standing awkwardly in one of the corners when my handsome registrar invited me to initiate myself. I accepted enthusiastically, admitting my ignorance of the procedure, and was grateful when he agreed to show me what to do. A nurse arranged a trolley with all the bits we would need, and Adonis and I approached the patient's naked groin.

I put on a pair of sterile gloves. 'Now,' Adonis instructed, 'one hand is clean. One hand is dirty. With your dirty hand, swab the penis.' Struggling to prevent the words 'dirty' and 'penis' from conjuring certain private fantasies about myself with this surgeon, I began to blush. I washed the man's glans.

A small coterie of theatre staff were enjoying my clear discomfort, as my registrar continued. 'Now, with that hand, hold the penis still. And with your clean hand' – a breeze of relief at not having to keep hearing the word 'dirty' lightened my blush here – 'take the lignocaine jelly and introduce it into the meatus.' What I now saw as my useless, trembling and woefully clean, never-to-be-meaningfully-dirty hand fumbled with the man's limp organ and the vial of jelly which I hoped would disappear into his penis poured out all over his groin. Adonis, from his lofty position of experience and romantic obliviousness, began to find my incompetence

amusing. 'Pull back the foreskin and introduce the catheter.'
No penis, all foreskin, the task seemed impossible. The
slippery prepuce appeared to have no underlying structure
to be retracted on so that the end of the foot-long catheter
kept popping out of the baggy eye of the man's penis,
flicking jelly around with every jaunty boing. Nurses and
theatre underlings tittered. Adonis woundingly quipped, 'I
thought you might have been better at this. Not your first
penis, surely?' 'My first floppy one, yes!' was all I could
hotly reply.

Adonis eventually finished the job for me, but for weeks
afterwards I was greeted in operating theatres the hospital
over with sniggers from senior surgeons, identifying me
as the one who had declared herself used to handling
firmer members.

Another awkward encounter, which made me feel like
I had been cast back to peripuberty, occurred during an
on-call. I was asked to see a post-operative orthopaedic
patient suffering from what is known as phimosis. This
is a painful condition which occurs if the foreskin is pulled
back over the head of the penis for any length of time.
The band of retracted skin acts like a tourniquet, impeding
drainage of blood from the penis and causing it to balloon
painfully. In hospital, it may happen when a nurse or
doctor has forgotten to pull a foreskin back into position
after inserting a catheter.

It was the middle of the night when I arrived on the
orthopaedic ward and I was immediately able to make
out a low groaning, separate from the ward's collective
groan. Steve, the burly chief nurse, led me to Mr Ashton's
bed, drew the curtain around me and the patient and,
with an encouraging wink, left us to it. Leg and cast on

a pillow, Mr Ashton's head was thrown back in disquiet. His swollen, discoloured penis lay like a dark lighthouse against the horizon of the sheet's edge.

He was a young man. We were contemporaries. I tried to chase from my mind the idea that, in other circumstances, I might have met him at a party. I found myself perversely grateful that his pain left no room for embarrassment between us. He looked wildly at me and whimpered a little. I began to talk to him in a quiet voice, not because it was night-time but because I wanted him to look at me and think me quiet and therefore gentle, since what I began to explain to him was that I was going to put his sore penis into my hand and squeeze it. As soon as I said 'squeeze', I added 'very very gently', but what I didn't detail was that I would then start to squeeze it harder and harder until I chased all that pooled blood back up more proximally so I could get the foreskin noose loose and put things back where they belonged.

I took his next whimper for assent and, like someone on slow spool, finger by finger, enclosed as much of the head of his penis as I could in my hand. It felt as if the two of us were hardly touching. Mr Ashton drew breath at this point, his worst fears of vengeful womanhood perhaps allayed. Then, gradually, I began to apply more pressure, first just enough for the small muscles of my hand to relax their still semi-extended position, then more. In a curious inversion of other similar contacts, I felt rewarded as the contents of my grip began to shrink. I carried on applying pressure bit by bit. After about five minutes, I was clenching Mr Ashton's penis with all my might. As all the remaining trapped blood migrated northwards from the end of his organ, the young man's discomfort eased and what had previously looked like agony gave way now to nude shame. In the artificial dusk of the ward, we were suddenly just two young strangers, one holding the other's penis.

Mr Ashton said thanks and clearly couldn't wait for me to leave. I felt satisfied with a job well done but also wanted to make myself scarce. Steve made some obvious joke or other on my way off the ward and another task called me elsewhere.

The penis also makes its presence felt more subtly in the medical workplace. Before I had even thought of becoming a doctor, while studying English up north, one of my tutors sought the help of his surgeon brother to refurbish his kitchen. The evening this constructive individual arrived in town, I was at a small student dinner party at this tutor's house. We were eating meat and his brother ate a lot of it. We were telling young person's stories about our gap years, about the only adventures we had ever had, postcard-sized. His tales of cutting and thrusting in the operating room made ours seem small and silly. This Mr Silk had a few photo albums in his car, which he showed us over coffee. They were full of before-and-after pictures of tumours followed by smooth expanses of flesh; compound fractures followed by straightened limbs with neatly stitched skin. At the end of the meal, Mr Silk peeled an apple in front of us all, and we watched as a regular ribbon of skin eased its way from the fruit in a perfect, unbroken coil.

At twenty-two, I was amazed, so when a full evening of my attention was rewarded with a singular invitation to visit my tutor's brother in his operating theatre whenever I might next be in London, I accepted without hesitation.

DIRECT RED

Less than a month later, I took the train south one weekend to stay with an aunt. On the Saturday, I arose at dawn and caught the first tube to Mr Silk's private operating suite. I felt a great sense of excitement as I was shown to the women's changing room and handed my first ever surgical scrubs and cap. I remember as new the oddly industrial smell of the fabric, like hard dusty tarmac. And the feeling of being almost undressed, with only the starchy top and bottoms to brush against skin and underwear.

When he saw me, Mr Silk hugged me to his chest, then welcomed me into his theatre with exquisite grace. I was introduced to his urbane anaesthetist and his various helpers. He showed me what everything was. I mistook this for courteous surgical convention. It would take me fifteen years from this point to reacquire the feeling of being 'someone' in theatre, for more authentic reasons.

He then performed an athletic and dramatic hip replacement. I don't recall much of the procedural detail, complete neophyte as I then was. What has remained is a more sensate memory. The music of the anaesthetic equipment, heard for the first time with its hums and peeps and sighs. The mixed aroma of clean hard surfaces and the loam of the body's upturned soils. The migrainous glare of the theatre lights. The pared-down gestural language between the players.

When the operation was over, the patient wheeled out, the orderlies gone, Mr Silk produced a bottle of champagne from the anaesthetic fridge, and he and I and the anaesthetist stood in theatre and drank it all from those small slush-white beakers that have corrugated sides and usually hold children's squash. Knowing nothing of the mores of private medicine, I took this for surgical common-place, a kind of post-sacrificial bonding.

Afterwards, my tutor's brother took me out for lunch, and a sense of wonder and excitement and exhilaration at what I had seen poured from me limitlessly throughout the meal, so that all potentially awkward moments were smoothed by its unction; so that any opportunity to realise that it was a little odd to be sitting with this strange man in this restaurant in this way was lost in the sparkle of a surgical world newly seen, compared to which the normal world appeared foxed like an old photograph.

As we left the restaurant, he ushered me with his large all-doing hand upon my elbow, a hand which still gave off a faint scent of Betadine, between the two heavy wooden doors leading out of the restaurant to London and its usual traffic. He stopped me. He stood very close and said, 'It was a wonderful morning.' And then, 'My wife doesn't know about this.' Which seemed an odd preamble to a sudden sense I had that he might be about to put his large 55-year-old mouth on mine. I took a step back, and quickly opened the door leading to the street. After a stilted thanksgiving, I was walking to the Tube, and thence to my aunt's house. I was never given such special treatment again.

All workplaces are full of this. But in a career where the body is the common currency, it feels odd to have one's own body be at all the issue. However, if this kind of experience makes one self-conscious, far more disturbing is the situation where one's own romantic feelings about a patient get in the way.

As I was shaking out a new white coat from its flat-pack, to do my first on-call as a qualified doctor, on the other side of London, a perfect young bricklayer was accelerating his 750 cc motorbike to 60 mph on a seemingly empty city road. As the first hours of my on-call disappeared in little tasks and chats, he saw too late the van which pulled out from a side street and knocked him off his bike. While I wondered if the night had any excitement in store for me, Mark hit the ground, bounced several times onto all sorts of different bones, which broke, and then skated noisily across the gravelly surface of the road. He covered a hundred metres of this surface in ten seconds. He then lay silently in a heap for five minutes while the ambulance called by the man in the van came to fetch him. Soon afterwards, he reached A&E, where a trauma team was waiting. The primary survey of airway, breathing and circulation pronounced him alive; the secondary survey, where a quick run-through of every part of the body is performed, concluded that this man would be admitted to hospital as an orthopaedic patient, and that all other injuries would have to wait until the life-threatening bone ones were sorted out.

Mark had thirty-six fractures. Some of these were large single breaks, others accounted for by a single bone having shattered in several places. Amazingly, his skull and face had not been squashed and his internal organs had received no major injuries. His crash helmet and bones had served their purpose.

Two consultant orthopaedic surgeons, each with a registrar, took him to theatre and began to put things back in place. One I didn't know. The other was called Santa for his gut and facial hair and ho-hoing manner. He always called himself a carpenter and he certainly had his work cut out here. A big man, he began to straighten crooked limbs in order to stem the bleeding in and outside the bones that was threatening the young man's life.

I was summoned as the underling whose job it was to remove as much as I could of the gravel that had got stuck to Mark's grazed body and face when he came off his bike. For this, I was given a large plastic bowl of soapy water and several scrubbing brushes, the ones we use to clean our hands before operating. They have hard, densely packed plastic bristles and I felt quite sick as I was encouraged by Santa to rub ever harder, until several brushes had to be replaced by new ones, until the already so damaged man bled in response to my personal assault. Santa reassured me that I was doing my patient a favour, reducing his risk of infection and of the skin scarring that gravel causes, known as tattooing. So as I scrubbed, he bled and it seemed as if, within this room, we were exchanging deformity for deformity. The twisted limbs were straightening to calm the eye but the whole body was now looking veiled with the blood that my work had drawn from it. After a few hours, I left. I had worn four scrubbing brushes flat and my night on call was over.

The next time I saw Mark was on the intensive care unit the following day. His extremities were covered in plaster. External fixators stuck from various aspects of these casts like outsize Meccano scaffolds. Only stripes of skin were visible against the white and these looked swollen, their surface scuffed by my efforts. The young man's head was round with oedema. Round like a child's picture of a head. Not round like a head really is.

I was feeling a bit queasy. It was my first time on an ITU. I was still getting used to my white coat, which I wore awkwardly like someone trying to suit the wrong fashion. I was thinking I couldn't believe I was a doctor now and that I really didn't know what I was meant to be doing. I had a clipboard with all my consultant's patient names on the front piece of paper. There was a stout box next to each name in which I was meant to write the jobs that would need doing that day for each patient. I held my pen above Mark's box, waiting for instruction or inspiration, and I peered at the man's face with what I hoped would pass for clinical scrutiny. His black, heavy-lidded eyes were open a little, like a turtle's, and I saw the globes within them turn in my direction. The half-dead man looked at me and he winked. My heart contracted slightly and my palms prickled. I looked at my colleagues but they were all involved in constructive decision-making. When I glanced back, Mark had looked away.

For the next six weeks, I saw Mark every day and during many nights. I talked to him more than to anyone else. This was my first house job, back at a time when the hospital gave you a bedroom for twelve months on the assumption that you'd be working too many hours a week for it to be worth going home. I saw very little of my friends outside medicine during this time. And Mark's friends visited him for a week or two until the thrill of his accident gave way to the mundanity of watching him heal.

So, we became friends. He was the one to give me reassuring looks when I was being humiliated with difficult consultant's questions on the ward round. He was the one who often encouraged me, at three in the morning, to stop working for ten minutes to have a cup of tea. He who asked me how trying to become the doctor I was, was feeling. Who told me I was good.

And I filled a gap for him too, the line between my clinical and personal questions blurring daily. I only realised how odd things had become when a nurse asked me one day if I could check Mark's catheter since he had been experiencing some discomfort in his penis and I confessed, to my shame, that I couldn't do the job. I just knew him too well. Luckily, the nurse understood and asked someone else.

As a healthy woman in my twenties, I could not help but notice that, as Mark got better day by day, he was transforming from the swollen-headed broken thing I had first observed into a guy who was the spit of the young Marlon Brando. With his facial swelling down, Mark was beautiful and, when I remembered that early wink in the ITU in the context of the man who was now in front of me, I felt confused. I started thinking romantically about him, despite myself. I began to dread and long for the time when our ortho round would stop at his bedside. I felt unduly self-conscious if Santa asked me a medical question in front of him that I couldn't answer. I spent one horrible afternoon hovering on the ward trying to work out who exactly his young female visitor was, and what relationship he had with her.

Things reached a climax one night when I was covering all the ortho wards on call. It had been a busy night and I had spent much of it in A&E helping out with two trauma patients. The last of these had come in fresh from a road traffic accident and had died soon after arriving in hospital, despite our efforts. It was about five in the morning and my bleep had mercifully stopped bleeping. Usually, I would have gone up to my room, chased the cockroaches out and lain down for an hour or so's sleep.

On this day, though, I was feeling jangled by the night so I decided to go to the ward to see if Mark was awake.

I found him sitting up in bed leafing through a motor-cycle magazine with his spare, uncasted arm, though so little light was penetrating the dirty window by his bed that I wondered how he could see the pictures, let alone read the print. 'You look shagged out,' he said, addressing my by my nickname, which he had now been using for a couple of weeks when we were alone.

I sat down and told him the bare bones of what I'd spent my last hour doing. Pumping a man's chest. Feeling his ribs break beneath my hands. Knowing that this didn't really matter because he was dead. Seeing the colour of his skin turn grey amidst the medic-ripped clothes.

Handsome, Mark faced me with such affection. In the semi-darkness, he did nothing to attenuate the feelings in his face. I looked at his eyes and the thing that usually buffers people's glances when they look at one another fell away and a warmth spread through my chest and made me feel my heart inside me.

Mark's arm and hand, resting on the pillow and then the motorcycle magazine, looked strong. A real workman's hand, not like Santa's. Lovely fingers, proper veins. Muscles still there despite the long bed rest. He lifted his hand from where it lay on the magazine and with a movement that didn't require him to shift much at all, he lifted up the bedclothes and held them about six inches above the mattress. He held my glance, and his eyes and his gesture invited me into his bed.

The gesture was so in tune with everything that had gone before, so welcome after the night I had had, that I actually felt my quadriceps muscles tense with the intention my legs had of lifting me from my chair and into the narrow bed alongside him, to feel him all along me. As my body leaned momentarily towards him, everything seemed to dilate. Then, when instinct halted me and I relaxed back in my seat, a disappointment lay between us.

We both looked away. I heard one of us sigh and when we looked at each other again, it was with a slight smiling sadness. I reached for the hand of his that had made that wonderful opportunity and I squeezed it like I knew a doctor could, hoping that the squeeze would convey all my most undoctorly feelings. Then I got up and went to my room. There I cried. Then I slept for a bit before getting up for the next ward round that morning.

We were both different after that. Mark was getting better and I stopped by to see him less often than before. For his part, he engaged me less, too. Seldom looked at me when I walked through the ward, drew me in less when I had reason to see him for something.

On the morning that he left the hospital, I was helping in clinic and when I went up at lunchtime to write blood results in the patients' notes, he was gone. I felt the anger of a jilted one before castigating myself. The next day, a crackly bag with a mother of pearl-coloured surface arrived on the ward with my name on it. Inside was a nest of pink shredded tissue paper and within this some luxury bath products. What you might give to an old lady, but sweeter. As if he were saying, this is an acceptable present but, between you and me, I am thinking of you in the bath. I still have an unopened soap from this set at home.

This is a hospital season. Things don't stay like this for long. You get used to handling patients' genitals so that the only mental shift you have to make is at home, to remind yourself in your personal life that your own private dealings are not meant to be practical. With time, your elders seek you out less often for their own romantic distraction. With fewer hours at work, you don't have the same intense relationships with patients. But, this initiation into hospital adulthood is useful to have. It brings you down, and makes a fool of you if you try and stand above those you are treating.

DEATH

Obstetrics was the subject I enjoyed least at medical school and no task was more laborious than consolidating an acceptable labour-ward logbook. To this end, each student was required to deliver ten babies and, to ensure there was enough raw material to go round, we were farmed out to various hospitals outside London. So one winter I found myself boarding at what used to be the Victorian Sea-Bathing Hospital in Margate and cycling into the obstetric department every day to take up my grudging station by the beds of its labouring women.

It took me a month to fulfil my quota of deliveries and I didn't much enjoy the time. I resented being at the mercy of the midwives, who seemed intent on punishing anyone who was or aspired to be a doctor. I was exasperated by how long it took for the truly productive part of labour to get under way. I was embarrassed by the high emotion and a little sickened by the sheer physical rawness of it all. And I suppose I was disappointed to find that, unlike all the other medical students, I did not feel profoundly moved or tearful at the point of a child's entry into the world. On the whole, I wanted a signature in my book and to get as far away from the hospital as possible.

What this month did achieve, however, was to give me a due sense of the momentousness of life's beginning. But nothing in our medical school curriculum performed an equivalent function for death. In biochemistry and physiology we learned about apoptosis – or programmed cell death – and the minute processes by which the body renews itself; in pathology we noted the morphology of such events under a microscope. But essentially, death was packaged as the ultimate point of failure, the consequence of disease prevailing over medical and surgical industry. We did not sit by ten deathbeds to mirror those ten births; we did not learn of final rot the way we learned of miraculous growth.

Accordingly, whatever I gleaned about the human aspect of what happens when someone dies seemed to come to me randomly and privately. My experience began in the dissecting room, a place where I was to spend Monday and Thursday afternoons for the first two years of my training, dissecting cadaver number sixteen.

Mixed feelings accompanied my initial day there. The scent of formalin and decomposition was as off-putting as I had been told it would be, but the prospect of the unveiling that awaited me was alluring. I remember huddling around the door with a hundred or so other medical students and noticing how socially awkward we had become, flirtatious almost, like a group of young people hoping to gain access to a humourlessly selective nightclub.

And in some way, I expected to enter that sort of self-consciously lugubrious environment, somewhere spooky, a suitable landscape for the Grim Reaper, that had hitherto occupied my imagination. Instead, the door opened on a scene of loveliness. The room was in the Victorian style, with lots of wood panelling, and its high windows were thrown open on a blue sky. Within this room were what looked like nine chrome bunk beds, perfectly spaced in three rows as if for a giant's game of noughts and crosses.

Our anatomy lecturer's appearance was not so immaculate: a bearded man, his white coat a relief map of guts, he looked like a living Sweeney Todd. He explained the system to us, the mores of this particular small space. The double-decker trolleys each held two bodies. A simple lever system enabled one to rotate the two platforms so as to choose which body went on top. This meant two different classes could use the tables on different days. In groups of nine, we were allocated a cadaver, ours to dissect in tightly scheduled stages over the next two years. At the foot of each table was a bucket into which we were instructed to deposit any piece of flesh – however small – removed during dissection. At the end of the class, these buckets were emptied into nine metal drawers, numbered according to cadaver, so that at the end of two years, a decent and unhybridised burial or cremation could be performed for each person.

Another character who coloured this curious social scene was Bernard the technician. An ashen man, he was in charge of the anatomy room, and present during all our dissecting sessions. Sometimes he appeared at the end of the afternoon carrying a bucket of stinking formaldehyde and a large paintbrush with which to daub all the bodies before we wrapped them up in plastic at the end of a class. On other occasions, he sat in his corner of the room meticulously preparing prosections for future medical students to revise from. These are discrete parts of the body – limbs, heads, thoraces, pelvises – expertly dissected in layers to expose important structures which serve as useful practical specimens from which to learn. When doing this, Bernard always smoked and often had a can of John Smith's bitter sitting next to him or even inside the body part which was that day's project.

The only time I ever spoke to Bernard, he told me with tears in his eyes about a recent visit to the dissecting room of a local veterinary college. He expressed his relief at not working amongst the animal dead and said the sight of so many horses' corpses had made him feel terribly sad. It was a poignant remark from a man who appeared untouched by similar feelings about his fellow man.

Surprisingly few morbid details remain in my mind from this time, amongst them the way pickled flesh first struck me. When a bar of chocolate melts inside its wrapper and then gets hard again and you take the wrapper off, there are usually creases in the surface which recall its softer form. So it is with the embalmed human. All elasticity is gone, as is the usual colour. In the case of our cadaver, the whole corpse was dun, apart from the hands, which were stained brown by deposits of bilirubin.

There were some gruesome moments too. One dark autumn day, we were due to dissect the lower gut, rectum and anus. Our study of the upper body had been completed in the previous year, so everything above the diaphragm had been removed over the summer, and we were now working from half-bodies, to keep things clean and organised. In order to get a good cross-sectional view of the alimentary canal, someone from each group was asked to saw sagitally the whole way through the half-cadaver, cutting the trunk lengthwise in two and separating the legs from each other. Bernard handed me a two-foot-long carpentry saw and, once a couple of the others had lifted the cadaver up so that its feet were pointing in the air, he told me to start sawing. At first, I felt the crude corrugated blade snagging against the body's scrotum. Once through the skin, I got more purchase and it was more like cutting wood. I might have been back in the school workshop again. When I had separated the two legs, I carried one of them to the sink – it was very heavy – and washed ancient, desiccated faeces from inside it.

The strangest aspect of this event was how it passed like any humdrum other, without shrieking or comment from anyone in the room. I found myself thinking about context. About how odd it was that my relatively arbitrary medical student status sanctioned an activity that in any other place would be construed as mad or evil. That I could just go home and watch TV after acts that in a different setting could as easily point to the asylum.

Mainly, though, I recall how quickly the dissecting room became like any other rowdy classroom, how death seemed to be so much at home here as to be part of the furniture. As students, we gathered twice a week around our dissecting tables as if for social dining. The fact of what lay on the table in front of us seemed almost incidental, eclipsed by the more pressing student preoccupations of love and lust and the next party.

The strong sense I had of death's rightful place in this environment was sealed at the end of two years by a dignified cathedral memorial service at which relatives of those who had donated their bodies were invited to sit alongside us, their butchers. We had never learned the precise identities of the bodies we had become so familiar with over many months, but a list of all their names was now read out. I remember sitting in my pew and wrapping each enunciated male name around the physical memory I had in my mind, to try it for size and fit, as if by this I would capture the essence of a man I had never met but whose body I had come to know more intimately than that of any other person in my life.

What I think dissection chiefly gave me was a sound training in the crucial skill of distancing oneself from a patient. That season seems the bookend marking the beginning of a whole shelf of experiences with death which failed to unhinge me. These ranged from multiple bedside certifications of death, post-mortems and visits to the morgue, to breaking bad news to elderly patients in a seaside hospital whose local nickname was 'God's waiting room' because of its high pensioner population. There were deaths in theatre and fatal cardiac arrests in hospital loos and corridors. There were also those brought into casualty, dead on arrival. But it wasn't until I met one particular ill young patient that I began to feel what is really dreadful about it. Death as the imposter, the unwanted guest, the Banquo.

During a night on call as a junior general surgeon, I was summoned to A&E to see a twenty-year-old man,

Troy, who had been waiting in the department several hours complaining of lower abdominal discomfort. He worked as a hip-hop DJ in Bradford but was visiting family in London for the week. He was beautiful: young, black, fit, slightly cross. Just the kind of patient to make me feel a little self-conscious as I took his history and examined him. Conversely, when he looked at me, he did so with indifference. He answered my questions briefly and intelligently. For a week, he had felt a constant dull ache below his belly button and had lost his appetite. Now, he was finding it almost impossible to empty his bowels despite a constant desire to do so – an unpleasant state known in symptom nomenclature as 'tenesmus'. He was generally fit and well and there was no other relevant history. Abdominal examination revealed a slight fullness in the left lower quadrant of the abdomen, which I took to be the consequence of simple constipation; digital examination of the rectum was also unremarkable. Basic observations and blood tests were all normal. I reassured him, told him to increase his fluid intake and sent him home.

Three days later, on call again, I faced Troy for the second time. He looked more uncomfortable than he had before but otherwise his story remained unchanged. A repeat examination did not reveal anything new. I felt an uneasy sense of my own diagnostic inadequacy: this young man was no malingerer, indeed he appeared almost ashamed that his fine young constitution was letting him down in some unknown way. I called my registrar and told him my thoughts. He came to review the patient and, unable to identify anything in particular, nonetheless shared my sense that something was not adding up, that the very presence of this Hercules in a hospital was worrying in itself. We went to discuss our patient with a radiologist and to seek the help of that great inanimate soothsayer, the CT scanner.

Later that day, in the depressing navy glow of the X-ray viewing room, we stood in front of Troy's pictures and heard the radiologist source his cause for complaint: a large tumour wrapped all the way around Troy's sigmoid colon, compressing it and almost preventing the passage of faeces into the rectum. Troy had significantly advanced bowel cancer, rare for a man of his age, and would need urgent surgery to bypass it before he went into complete bowel obstruction.

I went with my registrar to deliver the news to Troy. We found him alone in his hospital bed, although the ward sister said he had had lots of visitors that day. This curious combination of solitude and popularity was something I would come to associate with Troy as the days went by. Soon, he would allow no one but his mother to his bedside, but the flow of new cards and other bright missives never slowed. The corridor outside his ward had a certain convivial clamour until the day he left it. Sullen lovely girls loitered there, asking after him whenever I left the ward.

As doctors, none of us achieved much in the way of verbal exchange with Troy; understandably, I suppose, he seemed reluctant to make what was so hard for him easy for us. As my registrar explained the presence of cancer to Troy, his face looked dismayed but not surprised. A short silence followed the medical exegesis, then quietly from somewhere deep in the diaphragm, Troy began to produce a sound which I first took for a developing sob, but soon recognised as a kind of simulated drumbeat, a bass line, like the heavy woofer noise one hears from a souped-up car trawling the King's Road, kerb-crawling applause. His long toes kept company with this rhythm, but his eyes stayed with my registrar, following his description of what would happen next: a major abdominal operation the next day to try and remove his tumour.

We did take Troy to theatre and open him up. I felt ashamed at how wonderful it was to see anatomy so perfectly displayed; I am used to beholding the visceral soup of the middle-aged and unfit. What we found when we reached the site of Troy's tumour was an unwinnable situation. The cancer had twisted itself around all of his major abdominal vessels as well as his bowel and was therefore not resectable. His liver was stiff with metastasis. All we were able to do was take out as much as we could, a demoralising process called 'debulking', and form a stoma on his abdominal wall so that the faeces which could not pass through him in the normal way would have some exit.

It took him a week to die. This coincided with my turn to do a week of nights on call. From some guilty compulsion I cannot quite understand, I visited Troy every morning as my last duty before going home. Afterwards, I would cycle hard along the Embankment, feeling the pleasure of life and luck in my veins before settling down to scrambled eggs, juice laced with Pimm's, and a day of sleeping before the next night at work.

These visits were both ghostly and enthralling. After surgery, Troy was transferred to one of the isolation rooms at the end of the general surgery ward, privilege of the mad, the dangerously infected and the dying. The place always smelled foul because of all the gut problems, healing bowels and burgeoning stoma bags, but as I wandered down to Troy's room, I regretted the passage of this simple, discoverable alloy of odours. What replaced it was the smell of death. Acrid, full of the hormones of fear, of decay still fuelled by life. It was wintertime and the room was always in near darkness. I never found Troy asleep despite the early hour. I would walk through his door with a sense of dread and find him propped up in bed, every day looking sicker and wilder than he had the day before. It put me in mind of that Keats line from 'Ode to a Nightingale' about how 'youth grows pale, and spectre-thin, and dies'. I also remember the increasing gallery of cards which covered his hospital walls, a loving but somehow perverse pageant of get-well-soon messages from the family, friends and, I assumed, lovers whom he continued to keep from his bedside, his deathbed.

For six mornings, I entered the room, asked Troy point-lessly how he was, knowing I would receive no response. Offered water or a rearrangement of pillows. Felt awkward, gave cold comfort. And during each of these brief charades, I felt the heavy silent thrum of death all around me, scaring me to my heart. I wondered how this room, in which I had visited so many patients over the months, could ever feel exorcised after this. I was always more than glad to leave.

After my seventh night on call, I went to visit Troy for what I knew would be the last time. A week of nights for a junior doctor was always followed by a week of leave and I knew he wouldn't survive much longer. I entered his room that morning, therefore, with a mixed sense of relief that my nocturnal work sentence had come to an end, and trepidation that I would be saying goodbye to this particular patient.

As ever, Troy was sitting up in bed, as if in expectation. He looked emaciated and afraid, unrecognisable as the creature I had met in the emergency room a mere ten days or so before. I sat down next to him, and served him my usual platitudes. I then fell silent, unsure of how or when to leave, wanting somehow to signal that I wouldn't be back the next day because my night duty was over, without having to introduce into the conversation any notion of farewell, any provisional kind of ending, when death itself seemed so near.

As I sat there dumbfounded, Troy lifted one of my hands from my lap and squeezed it. He then put it back. He didn't speak or turn to face me. I left the room soon after, saying goodbye softly as I closed the door behind me. A week later, I learned that he had died that morning, just two or three hours after I went home.

In book six of Virgil's *Aeneid*, the eponymous hero goes on a tour of the underworld and comes face to face with signal dead people from his past. Before he can chart the way to the founding of Rome, he has to reconcile himself not only with loss but with personal incapacity, the little he was able to do to save these souls.

For some time in my early years of training, I had the uncomfortable sense that my encounters with death were having the opposite effect on me. That death was coming to me in such neat, timetabled parcels or in such strangely appropriate circumstances as to accentuate my very distance from it. To make me feel my otherness and vitality as a sort of professional heirloom.

To some extent, of course, good medical practice relies

on this sense of detachment. No one really wants their doctor weeping by their bedside; there is usually a job to be done. But, there are times when all our patients require of us is to be ourselves. And for this, we need to have felt the gap between a patient's approaching death and our own life as something less than controlled. During those last few mornings with Troy, what I mainly felt was shame. At my exciting life stretching ahead. At my ridiculous preeny white coat. At my uselessness as a doctor and companion. And in the end, I think this sense of my own smallness is the best I have had to offer at this – and many subsequent – deathbeds.

VOICES

Despite technological advances, the most useful tool available to a doctor remains their patient's voice. A person may not know the name of the disease they have but, by telling you their story, they will usually lead you to it. Part of this story may be delivered in the body's special language of physical signs, apprehended via observation and the doctor's examination. But of far greater importance are the patient's words, their speech, their voice.

If someone has no voice or no way of being heard, the process of diagnosing and treating them is very difficult. Sometimes this happens because a person is aphonic or unable to speak. In medicine, strokes, tumours and infections can all damage the area of the brain that produces words. In surgery, cancer may result in having to remove a patient's voice box or tongue. There are also psychiatric reasons for someone not being able to talk. At other times, a patient's voice may be present but incomprehensible. In these circumstances, new, oblique ways of communicating are often found.

I was packing things away in my bag one morning, pleased that clinic had finished early, looking forward to lunch. So when Janet the clinic nurse put her head around the door and said, 'Your last patient has just arrived. Transport came late to pick him up,' I said, 'Oh,' and thought 'Damn.' All I could hope now was that this unvouched-for appointment would be a quick one.

One glance at the set of notes on the shelf outside my consulting room made me realise that this was unlikely. They were thick like a phone book. My patient would either be medically complicated or a hypochondriac. Either way, goodbye lunch. I hoisted the slab of pages off the shelf and took it into my room for a quick look at the GP's letter of referral.

'Dear surgical colleague, please will you see this pleasant sixty-year-old gentleman with cerebral palsy associated with choreoathetosis. For the past six weeks, he has been experiencing constipation. Please could you rule out a serious cause for his complaint.' I felt an all too familiar sense of shame at my previous desire to get out of clinic and went to fetch Mr Dean from the waiting room.

I called his name. Two people, sitting next to each other, acknowledged my announcement. One of the men looked up at me. The other responded to my announcement with a strong, generalised writhing of the limbs, head and neck, and facial muscles, the movement disorder that the GP had mentioned in his letter. Choreoathetosis. From *chorea*, meaning dance. And *athetosis*, meaning incongruous.

The able man, whom I took for a porter or a nurse,

pushed the disabled man into my room. The doorway was narrow and the wheelchair was wide. But the real problem was that it was difficult for Mr Dean to keep his limbs within the confines of the chair. They flailed vigorously, banging into the corridor walls. The transmitted effort of his helper, the intention we all had to get him from A to B, seemed to agitate him and exacerbate his condition.

Despite years of medical training and exposure, I felt embarrassed by this man's lack of control. I didn't know where to look. I made some silly comment or other about the sluggish progress of the NHS wheelchair. I have no idea what Mr Dean's response to this was. His attender had a composed face and he also admitted nothing by way of expression. The comparison between the facial chaos of the one and the stoniness of the other was marked. Between them, shared out, they could have made two very animated faces. Two clowns.

Finally, they were both ready. Mr Dean's movements had abated somewhat but despite his efforts to look at me, his neck remained powerfully extended, his head rotating on it as on some massive pivot. As if in sympathy, his helper looked down, also not meeting my eye.

Briefly, I introduced myself, and since Mr Dean was still trying to compose himself enough to speak, I tried to make a connection with his associate. He, however, still refused to look at me. I pressed on. 'Your GP has written to me to say that you have been having problems emptying your bowels lately.' I knew from reading the notes that Mr Dean was in no way mentally impaired, had a degree even. Nonetheless, I found it almost impossible not to enunciate my words in a certain unmistakable way, like you do to a child or deaf person. I wonder if this is inevitable when you have no idea how your communication is being received. You feel like you can't be getting through.

Then, though, Mr Dean did start to speak. I had never heard a voice like it. His head was still thrown back. He was struggling to still it. His tongue was moving in and out of his mouth wildly. I looked at this tongue. Because it was coming so far out of his mouth, you could see much more of the length of it than you usually can. It reminded me of my pre-clinical days when I had first seen tongues, lined up on the slab, ready for dissection, and had realised how very long they are. In normal life you just see the front part, lying in the bowl of someone else's mouth or your own when you are brushing your teeth. Mr Dean's looked hugely muscular and a bit frightful.

The noises that came from Mr Dean had beginnings and endings and for this reason alone I knew they were words. But nothing else was recognisable. Not a single phoneme. Uncertain of what I would do next, I hoped this must be some sort of warm-up that would resolve into a language that I might be able to comprehend. I felt the awkwardness of not being able to do what you usually do when someone is in mid-flow, talking to you. You nod and raise your eyebrows and sundry other things that collectively say, 'Yes. Go on. I'm interested.' How could I do this when I understood nothing? How could I not do this without looking rude or blank or prejudiced?

I was about to ask Mr Dean's helper if he could fill in the gaps, when I noticed that this man's head was tilted slightly to one side like a bird's. And then he started to speak in a voice whose timbre seemed curiously in tune with Mr Dean's slurred noises. The frequencies seemed the same and the words were all drawn out in the same way.

'Yeeeees. It waaaas baaad. Buuut nowwww it's bettterrr.' The noises and the helper's enunciated syllables seemed to join and make one noise, like two people singing the same note, like woodwind players tuning up on an A. The word sounds of one and the unworded ones of the other sounded thick. Like how Rick Astley sings, as if his mouth is full of cake. Or like an echo would sound if it happened somewhere soft.

My relief at hearing that this patient's symptoms had already gone mixed with my desire to observe more of the sympathetic communication between him and his associate. Mr Dean started again, as if intuiting my thoughts. Apart from the pauses between the sounds, which indicated separate words, I could decipher nothing. Like an auditory amanuensis, the helper intoned, 'Thiiiiiiinngs gooot better when I caaaame offff the laast medicine.'

As he said this I could hear the patient say 'Yeeeeessss' and then the helper joined in and said 'Yeeeessss' too. It felt like a buzzing and a humming. They carried on like this, the two of them in harmony. And this put the relationship between me and them into relief. Usually, I have acknowledged an interpreter as separate from the patient they are assisting. They have recognised me too with a sense of our being on the same team, two players for the NHS side. What set this interpreter aside from any other I have known is that he seemed to be doing his best to efface himself as an autonomous player. To be refusing a dialogue with me distinct from my dialogue with the patient or even a communication with facial gestures. It was as if he was Mr Dean's voice.

This sense I had was emphasised at the end of the thankfully very short and straightforward consultation. The helper rose to push Mr Dean from the room and I said, 'Have a nice day.' The helper said, 'You too,' in a dysarthric voice as his charge mouthed grotesquely. This encounter stuck in my head as an example of how someone with no comprehensible voice can still find a way to make themselves understood.

However, sometimes patients are less successful at getting their message across. Even if their voice is fine, they may find it hard to say what they mean. Worse still are those situations when a patient's voice works beautifully and delivers a clear message but nonetheless is not heard.

One morning, I was consenting people for the breast surgery theatre list. One set of notes remained in the tray. I often find myself looking at the sticker on the outside of the notes to see what the date of birth is. Somehow, I imagine that a person is too young to be ill if they are born after me. This woman was only twenty-six. I immediately thought, oh she's probably having some little innocuous biopsy done, it's not likely to be anything big at that age. So when I looked her up on the computer so I would know what to consent her for, I was not prepared for what was planned: double mastectomy. God, I thought, as an image of my own naked breasts flashed before me.

My thoughts stopped when my hands found the right page in the notes. A letter from one of the general surgeons to the GP explained that Jane Manning had received a diagnosis of invasive ductal carcinoma of the right breast. She had been offered a wide local excision with axillary clearance of lymph nodes but had opted instead for a double mastectomy for the combined benefits of treatment and prophylaxis. Her mother had died of breast cancer at forty-five when Jane was just fifteen and she was desperate not to follow suit.

As I approached the relatives' room where I knew my patient was waiting, I glanced down at my own chest and was relieved to find it in something loose. I didn't want my breasts to show, to mock hers. When I walked in, though, I felt a sense of shame at the room in which she sat. It was yellow and the chairs were easy. A tactless Vettriano print on the wall showed a shapely woman dancing with her smart lover, while a lackey sheltered them from the invisible storm. She, the patient, was flanked on one side by a rack of leaflets bearing the title 'Your mastectomy' and some plastic flowers. On the other side of her was an older man, holding her hand in his hand in his lap.

She looked younger than she was and held her slim upper half straight like a dancer. She was wearing jeans and a long-sleeved grey T-shirt with a short-sleeved navy jumper on top, which looked like cashmere. I wondered if she had put her breasts in something so soft on purpose.

She wore no make-up or earrings. She had clear skin and eyes and her hair was pulled back from her face in a way that suggested she didn't need to make allowances. I thought that I would probably soon realise she was beautiful in that way that you sometimes do after a little pause. I introduced myself and sat down opposite her and the man I assumed was her lover, although she didn't seem to be leaning into him at all. Her body didn't respond specifically to my words. She had been ready since I came and simply remained so. But suddenly the vanilla room was alive with the noise that came from him.

'I am Philip Manning. I am Jane's brother.' His voice seemed to reach into every corner of the room in which we sat. Then he said, 'I am here to support her.' As he spoke, his eyes glittered and looked wide like the eyes of the dog in *The Tinder Box*, which are like windmills. In his already wide-open face. When I looked back at her, I began to distinguish that beauty I had thought would appear to me.

I explained, 'I'm here to tell you what we're going to do next week. To get your consent and to answer any questions you might have. Before I consent you for this surgery which I know you have chosen, I just want to remind you that we are able to do a much smaller operation for you if you would like.'

It would be wrong to say she moved her mouth as if to speak for I did not see this. Perhaps I just felt the air shift around her a little. In any case, Philip immediately jumped in and began to speak again. He gave Jane her hand back so that he could do this energetically.

'It may seem odd to you, Doctor,' he said in a slightly stagey way. 'Our mother had breast cancer. She fought a terrible battle and even though she had the tumour removed from one side, it still came back on the other. We've done our research and we've chosen this operation to make sure Jane survives this.'

She said and did nothing to disagree with her brother's pronouncement. I didn't want to make things worse for her by pushing her to speak if she didn't want to. I thought, all I can do is address myself to her, even if her sibling is speaking for her, even if he is her voice. So I turned to her and continued. 'OK. Well, it sounds as if you have given it a lot of thought. So I'll tell you what the operation involves.'

I detailed then, in terms as plain and unemotive as I could, that we would remove each breast in turn. We would send samples from each side to histology. Then we would close the defects. Immediately, I regretted using this automatic surgical word. Moving on, I explained that she would have drains coming out of her wounds when she woke. I then asked her if anyone had spoken to her about the future possibility of breast or nipple reconstruction.

Again, Philip spoke, 'We just want to get through all the treatment before thinking of the frills. We think that conversation is for much later.'

I was glad to pass the consent form over to her because I am quite sure he would have signed it for her if he could. She had a lovely hand, the writing and the fingers. I filed the form in her notes and was about to rise to leave the room when she opened her mouth and spoke. She did this quietly, but her words were precise. Each one had a pause after it, like a rest in a musical score. The syllables were like clear little bells. 'I have a tiny mole between my breasts. Right in the middle. Please, if it's possible to leave it there, could you?'

'Absolutely!' I replied with inappropriate cheeriness, because I was so relieved that she had actually asked for something, however small. Because she had spoken. I turned back to the consent form and in the section for naming the planned operation, next to where I had written the words 'Bilateral Mastectomy', I wrote in brackets, 'Please do not excise benign naevus on skin between right and left breast.'

The day of Jane's operation came and was sunny. I was to spend the morning assisting in theatre and then had the afternoon free for study. I had slept and eaten well and felt happy. 'On the Wings of Love' was playing on the theatre radio and staff bustled about getting everything ready. Checking instruments. Talking about weekend plans. I heard Jane arriving next door in the anaesthetic room, and then I heard the voice of my consultant, Mr Moore, introducing himself.

I went round to the sinks and slapped a sealed gown-bag up on the counter. Then I added one for the consultant and another for whichever registrar would be joining us. I pulled apart the two plastic sides and tipped out the sterile pack. I did the same with my size 7 gloves, emptying them from their cellophane casing on top of the green sterile square. Then I tied the two ribbons of my mask behind my head and squidged the metal strip over my nose, which is like the bit that keeps the top of rubbish bags twisted, so that my face was snugly covered.

I turned on two of the six long-armed taps, arranged in three pairs along the wall-length sink, and adjusted them so that the stream of water that came out between them was the right temperature. I wet my hands and squeezed Betadine onto them by pressing the dispenser with an elbow. The radio was now playing 'One' by U2. By the time the song was in full swing, I had finished washing and had unfolded my gown and put it on along with the gloves. One of the scrub nurses was behind me fastening the ties all the way down the back. I thanked her and moved into the main room of theatre, hands crossed over my chest to preserve sterility.

The doors smacked with the sound of the anaesthetic

gurney being pushed up against them and there she was, lying asleep on her back, arms by her sides. She looked as if she was already in her coffin. Except for the grace which animated her even in repose. Naked from the waist up, her slimness was pronounced. The outline of ribs could just be seen beneath her skin which was as clear as the skin of her face. Her breasts looked very small with her in this position, falling back into her narrow chest. I felt a tightness in my throat, which made me wonder if I was about to cry, although I had never wanted to cry in theatre before.

Then my heart really sank as I made out the unmistakable trilling voice of the female registrar whom I had been hoping would not be in attendance that day. Lucy Treacher, my least favourite surgeon ever! People often say that female surgeons are harder to work with than men. That they have had to be so tough to get to the top, that they are painfully exacting, especially with their female protégées. Personally, I have not found this. For me, this she-villain was one of a kind.

She came through from the anaesthetic room with our consultant and flashed me one of her smiles for his benefit. She had on her perfect make-up. Heavy black eyeliner, pink candy blush, lip gloss that highlighted her whitened smile. She was a tiny-framed, big-breasted young woman and she had a way of setting herself off to advantage. She wore her scrub top small and snug. Her bottoms were loose and rolled up at the bottom. The combined effect was that she seemed girlish and voluptuous all at the same time.

As the two of them scrubbed, I began to prep the patient. I was handed a swab on the end of the shiny tongs and dipped this into the bowl of brown Betadine.

I then painted Jane's chest, up to her neck, down to her navel. I did this gingerly, noting her tiny mole, making sure I didn't hide it with too thick a layer of dark, antiseptic paint.

By the time I was unfurling the drapes to cover her head and abdomen and leave only the square of her chest available for view, Lucy was by my side, nudging me over with a carefully placed elbow. All the while, she continued to deliver to the charmed consultant a description of her excellent performance at clay pigeon shooting the weekend before. 'To be honest, I was a pretty good shot all round, Mr M. But my favourite was the rabbit trap. I just imagined all the clays were real bunnies and suddenly I was on fire! Blowing all their furry little heads off!'

Mr Moore emerged tall, smiling and delighted from the scrub anteroom, his strong arms outspread to keep his gown from falling off as he waited for the theatre nurse to do it up. He looked like he wanted to kiss his scrumptious little registrar for being so violent. Not unusually, he had not acknowledged my presence once by this time.

Preparing to redo the job I had already done, Lucy asked the nurse for another swab and soaked it in antiseptic. She then pulled it roughly across the sleeping girl's chest so that every time she released the pressure at the end of a horizontal sweep, Jane's breast bounced back to its original position. I felt embarrassed to see this slightly alluring sight before our six eyes. I also noticed that, as Lucy paused mid-sentence to look at Mr Moore, a small pool of Betadine collected around where the swab rested on Jane's chest. And that when she continued chattering and cleaning, this pool remained and soon dried so that the dark patch of brown obscured the less brown mole that Jane had mentioned to me the previous week.

Mr Moore made some rudimentary pen marks around the patient's breasts and then, asking for the knife, began to make the first incision. Dainty Lucy had pleased him. He said that he would do one side and she could do the other. Soon, Jane's right breast had been outlined by the knife, highlighted in a dripping red ring. Mr Moore positioned two skin hooks and passed them to me to hold, to tent the skin upwards so that he could progressively detach the breast from the chest wall. He did this with diathermy scissors, which look like small nail scissors with a wire attached to the back of them. When the blades appose, they cut and cauterise at the same time.

He was slick and within ten minutes the breast was attached by only a small pedicle to Jane's body. By now, my skin hooks had proved unequal to the task of holding the dissected tissue out of the consultant's way. I was holding her breast all squashed and a bit crumpled in the palm of my hand. Blood trickled in a stream down the inside of my wrist onto the plasticky gown, and then dripped off me and onto the drape. It collected in a green valley and was congealing there like a small garnet jelly.

I lost my balance slightly as the breast was cut off. It was like being in a miniature tug of war at the point when you fall back and realise you are on the winning team. The scrub nurse passed a shiny kidney dish to me and I placed the breast in it. I attempted to unfold it as I did this. For some reason, I wanted to deposit it in its comeliest form.

Then, I looked back down again and felt peculiar.

Mr Moore was applying the diathermy forceps to the last oozing vessels and soon the area was dry. This red, dry circle looked flat on the operated side, like a child's chest. And the other side, with its remaining unsevered breast, suddenly looked round and womanly. But now the creature beside me was limbering up for her turn. It was the first time she had been quiet all morning. And I knew that now was the time that I should mention the issue of Jane's mole.

I had not spoken one word that day, so I cleared my throat. This sounded rude, as if I were grabbing long-solicited attention. Both my seniors turned to me in surprise as I made the noise and I said, my voice sounding very loud and resonant like someone talking on a learn-a-new-language tape, 'Did you see the bit on the consent form about her wanting to keep her mole?'

I don't know whether Mr Moore had been intending to move away at that point anyway, to show Lucy that he trusted her to get on with the next stage herself. But it seemed as if, as soon as my voice came out, he went to sit down. But 'Oh yes,' chirped she, 'I pointed your note out to Mr Moore just before we came through. We thought it was sweet that you were taking such an interest, although it did seem like rather an unorthodox use for the consent form to use it to describe the patient's little fancies. Are you sure you're in the right business, darling? You'd make a lovely GP.'

With that, she picked up the knife and held it towards the perfect blue ink sphere she had drawn around Jane's remaining breast. The dark ink line of her intended incision went right through the mole like a bypass through much-loved countryside. Her fisted hand was small and neat, the latex of her glove taut against her like sealskin. The blue line ran red as the blade stroked Jane's chest.

Silent again, I took two swabs and pulled them in opposite directions against the line as she cut through it, to ease her path. The fleet knife was now close to the middle of the sternum and I realised what I needed to do. I made sure, as I anticipated the arrival of the scalpel with my adjusted swabs, that I interpreted the line she had drawn to my own advantage and I put one of my swabs down so that its very corner lay over the mole. Almost as soon as I had done this, along came that sleek edge and slit just a mere breath away from the tiny mark I had defended. A disproportionate sense of relief stung my eyes. And the rest of the operation happened in a blur. Before I knew it, Lucy was securing two drains under the skin with tethered sutures. We were done.

I did not speak to Jane again. The conversations that took place on the ward rounds were usually between her and Lucy, and were about the amount of blood in her drains and, increasingly, when she could leave the hospital. And my shiny registrar was the surgeon who had removed her cancer. I would not have asked about that mole in any case. Perhaps her request had just been some sort of anxious reflex, some need on her part to say something in that room with her brother that day. But I was pleased with myself. I had saved for my patient the only thing she could bring herself to mention, the tiny mole that made her feel she would know herself, even after such therapeutic savagery had been performed.

Of all the disabilities a person may endure, perhaps none is more devastating than losing the power of speech. Aphonia is linked with a high rate of psychiatric morbidity and even suicide. Certainly, it is hard to doctor someone who has no voice. It is with words that patients are able to convey their needs, to let us know if we are helping them or not.

For these reasons, elaborate mechanisms for voice restoration exist in hospitals. There are mechanical, hand-held devices for laryngectomy patients or tiny latex Blom-Singer speech prostheses. There is a whole clinical discipline, known as speech and language therapy, devoted to this area.

But both the triumphs and the defeats of clinical communication may lie outside this remit. Sometimes, patients find their own significant ways of making themselves understood. And at other times, we doctors may deny our patients a voice through the unconscious but still brutal act of just not listening to it.

BEAUTY

From my earliest days at medical school, I found surgery not just practical but beautiful. Dating from that first operation, when I had seen my tutor's brother replacing a cranky hip joint with a new one, this sense of surgery's fine aesthetic gathered momentum during the early years of my clinical education. Compared to the limitlessly difficult and ambiguous world of medicine, surgery was diagnostically clear. Relatively few surgical diseases were described, all of them concerned with quite definite abnormalities. Tumours, fractures, clots. Empirically true, touchable facts.

The operations designed to treat these frailties were also lovely in their combination of regularity with a magical kind of artistry. In surgical textbooks, I found difficult procedures dissected and laid out in stages. They suggested a craft which was repeatable, reliable and always dramatic.

DIRECT RED

This last fact mattered to me. Being a surgeon just sounded so much more impressive than being a physician.

But the feature of surgery that struck me as most beautiful was its almost military adherence to the principle of order. Surgeons started their days an hour earlier than their medical counterparts and did ward rounds quickly and efficiently. Diseases were easy to diagnose, leaving time for the careful planning of classic procedures, tweaked to suit the individual patient. These operations were then performed with marvellous precision. Cure was not guaranteed, but decisive surgery was often a person's best chance of reaching that goal.

I observed the objective correlative of this feeling in the immaculate layout of the operating theatre. The geography is of a main room with annexes. Most important of these is the anaesthetic room, where the patient goes to be put to sleep, so as to avoid the stress of seeing where they are going to be cut open. The prep room is another antechamber, where the scrub nurse sorts through the pack of instruments, each operation with its own pack, with its own designated tools. Then there is the alcove for scrubbing, with its zinc sink and shelves piled with plastic-packed gowns and gloves in all sizes, in waxy paper envelopes.

I had enjoyed watching the choreography that animated this space many times. The way the anaesthetic doors would open to deliver a bedded, tubed patient at the same time as the scrub nurse appeared with her trolley, like a hostess bringing out a science-fiction tea. And how the surgeon would enter centre stage, arms held aloft, gown billowing like a gust-filled kite.

I suppose I was in love, seeing beauty all around me

53

in my new surgical world. It would not take long for me to see that surgery is not always rosy, not always controllable and pretty.

I was due to spend the evening in A&E, shadowing an SHO on his night shift. As a mere student, I had no responsiblility. I was there to learn what I could and to assist the junior doctor I had been assigned to, in whatever way he saw fit. To get a feel for this environment that would soon be like home.

That evening I was with a junior doctor called John. He was a conventional tubby guy, but I remember how attractive he seemed to me. After all, he was a real doctor and, although I was due to become one within months, the chasm of experience and style seemed huge between us. It's funny how doctors go from being really sexy when you're not one yourself, to rather unsexy when you are.

Well, he was busy and at a loss as to what to do with me. So he suggested that I go and take a history and do an examination on a man he had just seen, who had come in with abdominal pain. As John was telling me what to do, he was busy organising an intravenous urethrogram on the same patient, a scan which I knew was routinely performed on those thought to have a kidney stone. I felt disappointed that I already knew the diagnosis on the person I was about to see. What was the point in reading an Agatha Christie story if you already knew who the murderer was? I thought, as I headed for cubicle five.

I paused just outside the cubicle curtain, to collect myself, and to check, in my *Oxford Handbook*, vade mecum of all medical students, what questions I needed to ask someone with abdominal discomfort. I saw the usual list of factors germane to any sort of pain: onset, site, severity, duration, intensity, character, relieving or exacerbating factors. Plus the relevance of bladder and bowel habit. Then, conscious of trying to look less awkward than I felt, I went in.

The couple I introduced myself to were Mr Cooke and his wife. He was sitting on the bed, and she was sitting on the chair beside it. Despite being in his late sixties, he was trim. Sitting back at a forty-five-degree angle had not produced a little roll of fat at his belt-line. His face was not the florid hue of the cardiopath; his measured breathing suggested good lungs. Only a double furrow on his brow indicated discomfort. That and the fact that his eyes were closed as if he was trying to narrow his sensory field. His hair was grey and thin but looked windswept rather than straggly. He was wearing khaki trousers. Not genteel chinos, but made of something thicker and more practical, like canvas.

On his top half, he wore a plaid shirt whose sleeves were rolled to just above the elbow so that I could see slim but sinewy arms, finished with large, strong hands. His knuckles were like big marbles, and his veins looked like tree roots, as if they wouldn't be soft if you pressed them with a finger of childlike curiosity. He was a slight man, but valour vied with slightness to be noticed first.

Next to him, his wife appeared almost buxom. She had a good bosom, and it had that stiff unified look that made it hard to imagine that it was composed of two soft breasts. She had brown hair that was only just beginning to grey. It reached her shoulders, and some of it was held from her roughened cheek with a clip, which might have looked absurdly girlish but didn't, because her eyes, which met mine the instant that I walked into the room, had a shiny sort of wisdom in them.

It was hard to see exactly what she was wearing, since the folds of this merged into the creases and swathes of that, but it was all dark and soft, in greys and greens and browns, so that she looked wholesome and foresty. She had a handbag by her feet which stood up by itself. One of the handles was upright and the other had collapsed to one side. And on her lap she had one of those old mauve and white Penguins that they now design mugs from, and this one was Virginia Woolf's *A Room of One's Own*. Mrs Cooke looked as if she had had such a room all her life, or as if she had never needed one.

Because she was looking at me, I introduced myself more to her than him. He had opened his eyes when I entered the cubicle, but had closed them again when he heard the words 'medical student', although with a kind smile. I might have felt put out, but Mrs Cooke, in the same measure that her husband had dismissed me, welcomed me with her response. She gave me the kind of look that a governess might give a child who has just washed their hands adequately, and she closed her book. She put it in her bag and then sat up, hands in lap to give me her full attention. Her hands too looked strong. The skin on them was chapped like a gardener's. I thought briefly of the minute unfair discrepancy: that a man's strong hands are alluring, but that beautiful hands in a woman are those that have done nothing.

She was patient with my questions, but we both knew that a diagnosis had already been made, so the interview felt sluggish. I dreaded the prospect of having to examine this dignified man in front of his owl-like wife. I didn't like to think of touching, let alone hurting the abdomen that lay under that soft shirt. An abdomen which in my imagination grew intensely white and private.

So I was grateful when, by some happy conversational torque, things turned from the medical matter in hand to a discussion of poetry. I cannot remember how this happened. It turned out that Mr Cooke was a retired professor of English literature, and once we left the subject of his own cranky body behind, to turn to what interested him most, he became quite animated. His wife explained that they were engaged in a marriage-long dispute about the comparative merits of Augustan versus Romantic poetry. It must have been a sort of harbour for they began to banter lightly about it now, he sometimes opening his eyes to praise Keats or Shelley, or especially Wordsworth, over her favourites, the champion of whom appeared to be Alexander Pope.

Mrs Cooke's face had softened and she was saying, 'Oh, for goodness sake, Charles, all those ghastly demonstrations of feeling. All that narcissism. How can you . . .'

And he was chuckling, despite his still-closed eyelids. He reached for his wife's hand and found it easily. Grasping it in midair, he gave it a sort of playful shake up and down while he addressed me with, 'My wife loves Pope with all his strictures and his order. Because she finds the chaos of the really great poets a bit too scary.'

I noticed their hands, which stayed within the joint grip they had made for a few seconds after his last quip. Her scuffed red skin. His bony fingers. The difference between them. Then they had to let go because of the discomfort of his having to extend his arm off the bed with no support.

I was trying to think of a way I could join in their

conversation when Mr Cooke's face suddenly seemed to fold in on itself, and an exclamation of pain rang from him. There was sweat on his face where there hadn't been before, and he didn't look good. I got up, tripping slightly on my chair, and rushed to find John or a nurse.

Within two minutes, Mr Cooke had been wheeled into Resus, his wife as near to him as she could get, given the sudden interest of all the doctors and nurses taking him there, expediting this short journey. The space was compassed in a matter of seconds. Then Mr Cooke was being hooked up to all sorts of things and people were saying how low his blood pressure was, how tachycardic his pulse. Even in my student ignorance, I could tell he was in haemodynamic shock, he looked so grey and unwell.

A senior A&E doctor, realising that the diagnosis of ureteric colic had been wrong, performed a quick abdominal ultrasound right there, and this showed that Mr Cooke had a leaking abdominal aortic aneurysm. Unless he was taken immediately to have this most major of all blood vessels in the body repaired, he would not survive the next hour.

At that point, I noticed several things at once. A nurse, calling theatre to prepare them. The sight of John in the background looking as if he was about to cry. The A&E registrar telling me that they needed extra hands in theatre, that none of his juniors were available, and that I should go and help. The bang of the A&E doors as Mr Cooke's bed was bashed through them to take him to theatre. The sight of his wife, still relegated to the outer circle of bodies, standing in Resus, as the bed and her husband disappeared down the corridor. Trying to compose herself. Waiting for someone to tell her what she should do, where she should go.

I took a shortcut to theatre and changed hurriedly. They need me! I thought as I grabbed a blue cap from the cardboard box on top of the lockers on my way out of the women's changing room. Because I was alone, I allowed myself to feel the great excitement of the surgery I was about to assist in. I knew the operation would be dramatic, but had no doubt it would work. I was glad to be a part of this drama, and felt good even to be wearing surgical scrubs, a sense of pride I confess I still have whenever I don this costume, even since it has become my habit. I slowed my step as I approached the emergency theatre, so that I wouldn't look breathless and uncool when I got there.

What I saw when I walked into the room shocked me and made me feel ashamed of my recent exuberance. There was a scrum of blue backs leaning over Mr Cooke on the operating table. He was neither undressed, nor asleep, but the men in blue were working on him. One was cutting his shirt off and others were leaning on him, forcing him to lie down, despite his efforts to rise up and scram. I saw his slim, muscular belly, that part of him I had been reluctant to expose half an hour before, and I noticed the little red Campbell de Morgan spots on his skin, just like my dad has.

Two men took one arm each. Other helpers brought armrests which were fixed to the side of the operating table with large screws. Then Mr Cooke's arms were forced down at his sides, an immoral arm-wrestle, one man fighting two. Once overcome, his arms were strapped in position like you sometimes see in old films about madhouses.

And there was the most dreadful noise. Mr Cooke, previously so self-contained, was roaring like a bear. Then, as he was defeated, loud man-sobbing. And then this patient, pinned down in a position that reminded me of the Crucifixion, was attacked again, from another angle. An anaesthetist moved in unseen from north of his head, and his futile flailing started again as he felt the insult of a thick needle being pushed into one of his bulging neck veins. This was the central line, through which he would be monitored, as well as the conduit for receiving drugs and fluids.

At the same time, two surgeons were daubing his narrow front with brown Betadine in massive painty sweeps. Mr Cooke's legs were kicking a bit and his eyes were rolling all around, their luminous whites blindly scanning the activities taking place upon his powerless body. I didn't know who either of the surgeons was, only that one was a consultant and one a registrar. They didn't know who I was either, but I was asked to scrub and became one of two assistants. I was told where to stand, on the patient's right-hand side, next to the other helper. On the opposite side of the table were the vascular consultant and his registrar.

The operation began with the swiftest laparotomy incision I have ever seen, the very first I had witnessed at that early stage in my training. In one concerted movement, the consultant literally sliced Mr Cooke open, from xiphisternum to pubis. His proficiency was marvellously apparent to me, his decisiveness, his knowledge of exactly how much pressure to apply to the large blade to penetrate skin and subcutaneous tissue, without harming any important underlying structures.

With another single effort, the boss hoisted the whole gut out of Mr Cooke's abdominal cavity and dumped it unceremoniously on my side of the table. This forced me, and the guy I was standing next to, to huddle together, to form a barricade with our two adjacent bodies, to stop the snaking mass of small and large bowel from slipping between us, or around either of us, onto the floor. Arms outspread, we held its writhing bulk and I will never forget the eerie movements it made, vermiculating in our joint embrace.

Looking down, I peered into the trough of Mr Cooke's emptied abdomen, and could see it filling with blood so fast that the outline of the gushing source was visible beneath the red meniscus. Like when you fill a paddling pool with a hose and it's half full and you can see a knuckle shape on the surface just above where the hose is. I had been given two huge suctions and was holding their broad snouts into the crimson depths, one in each hand. These pipes were doing such a strong job that I could feel the pull of them sucking at the blood, and I could hear no milk-shake slurping noise from them. They were not wasting time sucking up a cocktail of air and fluid; they were just hungrily sucking blood.

For the next minute or so, nothing seemed to happen. The clearing of blood could not keep up with the rate at which more flowed from the leaking aorta. I was remembering, from my cadaveric dissection days, the first time I had seen this enormous vessel. It is as thick as a walking stick and stands plum in the centre of the body. It even has the same handle-shaped curve as it leaves its origin in the heart. From there, it travels all the way through the chest and abdomen down to the pelvis, where it bifurcates into the leg-supplying iliac arteries. I knew from my recent studies how few previously undiagnosed leaking aortic aneurysms are survived.

As if abandoning hope that he was ever going to get a clear view, the consultant splashed in, holding a weighty instrument. When his hands resurfaced, they were empty because he had used this instrument to clamp the aorta. Then he asked for the Dacron graft, a piece of tubing to replace the leaking bit of vessel. This looked like one of those concertina-type tubes that plumb washing machines. I was given a huge retractor to hold to keep the abdomen wide open, and would remain like this for the next three hours.

During that time, repeated attempts to make the graft work failed. Each time the boss undid the clamp, to check the patency of the anastomosis, blood poured into the abdominal cavity again.

I confess that when at four in the morning the consultant announced there was no more he could do, my main feeling was relief. The hours in theatre had piled up against the thirty minutes or so I had spent with Mr Cooke in A&E, so that my short connection with him felt out of date. So that any sense of sentiment I might have had had been eclipsed by the drama of the night. And even the drama now felt jaded. I was just tired and my arms hurt from holding the retractor for so long.

No one had spoken to me during this theatre episode so, once we had all stepped back from our meddling, it was easy for me to leave quickly. I didn't want to see Mr Cooke's blood brim over, or to hear it disrupt the silence of new death with its splish-splash on the floor.

After changing, and on my way out of the theatre suite,

I happened to pass the relatives' room. Through the window inlaid within its wooden, school-style door, I could see the broad back of the vascular consultant, a trapezoid imprint of sweat on his scrub top. And then I heard the sudden, uncontrolled noise of Mrs Cooke's first exhalation of grief, as horrible as the last sounds her husband had ever made, while struggling to resist the anaesthetic. Unheard by him, as he had been by her. Standing outside the room, outside of that immediate extreme zone, I felt embarrassed by the noise before it saddened me. In the way that the sound of people having sex in a nearby hotel room might embarrass you before having any other effect.

Then I saw the top of Mrs Cooke's head, mostly obscured from view by the consultant's shoulder. She had got up and she must have been hitting his chest because I could see his back shaking a bit, and I could see movement from her shoulder. I was afraid to see her face. I was afraid she would see mine, just gawping there through the window. And so, since it was not my grief and had not been my operation; since I was feeling no ache from personal loss or personal failure, I walked on and I walked away. I went home, and I never saw any of those people again.

There have been many bloody nights since that one. So that bloodiness has not interrupted my sense of surgery's beauty. And so that I know that the ugliness of that night was not about gore. Nor was it about misdiagnosis, which I have since learned is quite common in cases of leaking aneurysm, and is sometimes unavoidable.

What was awful that night was that, in the name of saving Mr Cooke's life, in the rush towards an operation that offered the only hope of survival, this man was denied his last minutes of liberty. The short time he had left was taken from him, minutes he would probably have spent holding his wife's hand as I had seen him do so easily when I had been talking to them earlier that night. Instead, he was rushed off, to meet a terrified end in a strange and brutal place at the hands of people who – though they aimed to be saviours – became his executioners.

I still see the beauty of surgery all around me when I'm at work. In clear diagnosis. In methodical procedure. In the rudimentary environment of the operating theatre. In the rigorous magic performed by surgeons on patients, whose diseases are often cured by going under the knife.

But even the most righteous surgery can be ugly. Even the most necessary operation, in the best hands, can fail. And in the process of acting in a patient's best surgical interests, we may sometimes make the final moments of their life more terrible than they would ever have been had we left them alone to say their farewells uninterfered with, more wholly and with more grace.

HIERARCHY

Surgery takes a long time to learn. Five years of medical school are just the lead-up to an apprenticeship which usually runs into decades. Of course, there are lots of facts to remember, and cutting people is a craft best acquired carefully. But the length of training serves another important function. It ensures that, by the time you have any real responsibility, you aren't young any more. This getting old makes you more aware and therefore safer.

When I first went to medical school, I only had to imagine myself as a surgeon to feel a self-congratulatory thrill that lasted the whole day. I felt capable and couldn't wait to be given some control. Thankfully, this cocky time was brief. I soon discovered the full extent of my uselessness.

At the end of my first week at medical school, I stopped by the anatomy department on my way out to meet friends for the evening. I was there to collect a skeleton, mine to look after for the next two years. The cardboard box which held it was about a metre long, big enough to hold a femur. And about nine inches wide and nine inches deep. Inside was a skull, its jaw newly attached to the temporal bone by a tiny spring. You could hold the head in one hand and make the teeth go clickety-clack. And there was a spine, all the vertebrae strung together like beads. And then there were all the bones from one arm and one leg. The individual bones of the hand and foot were wired in place like the vertebral column. But overall, these bits were loose so that every time you moved the casket they found new macabre arrangements. I couldn't wait to introduce my old acquaintances to this desiccated new one.

The size of this container suited my pride in it, its lightness my joy. I took it from the medical school and onto the Tube. I glowed. I wished it was transparent or that it said 'skeleton' on the side. I wanted total strangers to invite me to reveal my occupational identity, I felt so excited to be doing this wonderful thing with my life. I completed my whole journey with no human interaction. Even giving the box its own seat next to me had not prompted curiosity. I picked up pace, therefore, at the prospect of meeting my friends, who I knew would take an interest in my show-and-tell parcel, whose interest would frame and set my choice of career.

I arrived at the pub and saw none of my friends were there yet, so I went straight to the busiest part of the bar, put my ignored charge on a stool, and ordered myself a drink. At this stage, I was hoping a stranger would chat me up so that I could divert his questions to my precious cargo. A middle-aged couple approached me instead. They paid for my drink and asked me to join them while I waited for my friends to arrive. I moved swiftly from pleasantries to the fact that I was a medical student to the proud proclamation that I was now the responsible guardian of a skeleton, real bones. I was all ready to shake the box so that it would give a tempting low rattle. I wanted to grasp the sides of its lid and let the top shudder from the bottom.

Just then, there was a commotion on the other side of the pub. The man I had been talking to went round to see what had happened. He looked like he would be good at sorting out a brawl. Almost immediately, though, he rushed back round to his wife and me. His T-shirt had come untucked from its tethering in his below-the-tum jeans. His belly showed hairily and his eyes looked like balls, not discs. He didn't know my name so simply exclaimed, 'Medical student! Come quickly.'

I followed him round. I saw a man lying on his back on the floor. He was still and straight. He looked like he was performing something. A magic trick. Or measuring an empty floor in a house he was about to buy, to see if his double bed might fit there. His hair had fallen with him and was not strewn from him. He had jolly socks on and his eyes were open.

A man I didn't know said, 'He was going to the bar and he just suddenly fell down like that. He's not breathing. I think he's dead.' I didn't know why he was talking to me, and was about to add my own non-sequitur and say, 'No, I don't know him either,' when I realised that a small crowd of people had gathered and that the couple I had made friends with were explaining that I was a medical student, without adding what I had not bothered to mention, which was that I had been in training for less than a week. Without telling them what I hardly knew myself, which was that I knew nothing.

I felt big, with everyone looking at me. I was a training doctor. How lucky that I happened to be in the pub that evening. With a complete lack of self-awareness, I kneeled by the man's head. I put my index finger against his neck to feel for a pulse, which at that time I didn't even know was the carotid artery. I also bent my ear to his mouth and indeed heard and felt no breath come from it. 'Call an ambulance,' I said, before sitting back on my haunches. I had no more knowledge of resuscitation techniques than anyone else in the pub. I sat there for some time. There was still no sign of my friends.

Then there was a siren, and lights flashing through the bottle-green pub windows and alert, strong men moving people aside and approaching the moribund man with their casks of oxygen and contraptions. A mask was fitted to the unconscious man's face, with a ventilation bag attached to it. A man in a green boiler suit began chest compressions. Cold air coming through the double pub doors and activity perked everyone in this dopey room up, except the one they were working on. They put the man on a stretcher and they were on their way out when my acquaintance announced to the paramedics that I was a medical student and that I had been fantastic. The green practical man looked at me quickly with what I took for a sort of recognition, gave me the bag and told me to squeeze it, as he had been doing.

Then we all went outside and, because I was still pressing the bag in what I hoped was the right way, there was nothing else for me to do but climb with the others into the back of the ambulance. I did think of my skeleton left behind. And my handbag. But these things didn't matter now. The rear doors had clunked shut. One! Two! And the ambulance was pulling away from the kerb. One of the green men was driving. The other was in the back with me. And the mottled man was in the thick of it all.

The journey was short. My first ever ambulance, no longer closed to me like the confessionals of Larkin's poem, lurched and smelled. I was facing backwards and there were no windows to look out of. Then we were at the hospital, the doors opening onto the cold scent of wet car park. I was still squeezing the bag at the head end of things. I needed to concentrate so the bag wouldn't fall off the man's face as we hurried into A&E. Next, I was inside my first ever resuscitation cubicle. Someone whisked the green curtain around us, and a whole new set of efficient people did things. A nurse put a lead jacket over my head. This reminded me of one of those painting pinafores you wear at nursery school when you are going to do a picture on an easel. But it was heavier because it was full of lead to protect me from any X-rays that might be taken.

I was impressed by the fact that there was very little talking despite the number of people and all the action, and I felt at the heart of this team. Efficiency and neatness often go together, but here they didn't. Two people vied with each other to get quick intravenous access. Each held one of the patient's arms straight and pushed needles into its soft fold, the antecubital fossa. Blood meandered down the man's arms and made tiny splashes of bright red on the grey lino floor. The mess was like snacks at a drinks party. On the counters were kidney dishes piled with bloody gloves, and plastic boxes laden with sharps and venflon stickers. And the landscape of the patient himself had changed too. His shirt was open and he had vomit on his neck. Cardiac stickers made a pin-the-tail-on-the-donkey map on his chest, and he had tubes protruding from him. It was odd to think that this cubicle had recently been clean and empty.

The patient still hadn't woken up, but the activity gave his very lifelessness a sort of momentum. Adrenaline and atropine, pushed in aliquots into his cannula, were part of this relay of hopeful assaults, as were brief periods of chest compressions and triple serves of defibrillation. Someone put electrical paddles on his chest and the team leader said, 'All clear, oxygen clear, ready,' and everyone moved backwards, reminding me of the stepping-out part of the hokey-cokey or the way a cast all step back before they take their bow at the end of a play. But our patient did not applaud us by recovering. At a certain point, the consultant asked each one of us if we were happy to stop and the flurry of attempts to save this life ceased. There wasn't a reverential hush like you see on TV, with everyone looking meaningfully at each other. Rather, the activity that had seemed to be about making a mess, was now directed towards clearing up. Yellow metal rubbish bins clapped their pedalled clap. Gloves came off. A nurse mopped blood and sick off the patient like she was cleaning a messy child. The consultant came over and told me the paramedics would take me back to where they had found me.

I sat between them in the quiet, slow ambulance, feeling a poignant and not unsatisfying sort of sadness, and they took me back to the pub where last orders were in, and my friends were waiting for me. My skeleton was there too, and looked inert to me now. It was only when the hopeful bartender asked me how things had gone, and I saw his disappointment at my answer, that I realised something that had escaped me in A&E. Namely, that I had enjoyed the show but contributed nothing. A few months later, a little more informed, I would realise that the only person who had had the opportunity to save that man had been me, in the moments after he had collapsed. I had not even known basic first aid, so had squandered the chance and a life. I didn't ever feel quite so proud of being a medical student after that.

Over a number of years, and with the passage of many deaths, I left this keen but ineffective self behind. Seamlessly, I began to make myself useful. Each hospital job brought new levels of responsibility, minute increases in status within the overall structure of things. And then one day, I realised I wasn't a junior doctor any more; I had risen significantly in the hierarchy and become a registrar. This happened one summery week, when the leaves on the plane trees around the hospital brushed together softly like so many pat-a-cake hands. At the end of the interview when I got my job, I was told I would do my first on-call as a registrar the following morning.

I rose early that day. Instead of putting on the theatre scrubs which I had always worn for weekends on call as an SHO, I chose the suit I had used for my interview. I also packed a briefcase, instead of my old backpack. I had been given it by my parents at Christmas the year before, and had mistakenly taken it into work once to be met with ridicule by my junior colleagues, for getting ideas above my station. This morning its stiff click seemed to fit.

I arrived on the ward and was greeted by one of my surgical friends. He and I had been SHOs on this very ward for the past year. He had also been amongst the dozen or so at the interview the day before, competing for the job I now held. I thought how odd it was that a chasm had opened between us in terms of seniority although there was no difference in our knowledge.

He reached for the notes trolley, which the most junior person on the ward round rolls from bed to bed. It has a little fold-out table for leaning on when writing. The metal sides are grey and tubular like the sides of boarding-school beds. They have thick shiny paint on them, so much that you can see rivulets of dry paint that was once wet. I know the feeling of gripping this surface like I know the feeling of wearing a bra, so that you're not aware of it any more. The table edge rests against your belt and you put the tubular sides in your hands and have to swerve it largely as you do a heavy supermarket trolley to get it to go where you want it to. He did this. He knew the map of the patients. His list reminded him of their date of admission, their presenting complaint, their progress.

As we stopped at each bedside, I had to keep reminding myself to behave like a registrar, to stand a little aloof and let my SHO do the chores. Perhaps a little posturing was all that was required. Certainly, it all seemed easy enough. The first several patients had tonsillitis or nose-bleeds, or were recovering from the previous day's general ENT list. I had seen other registrars lay out simple plans for these things many times.

But then I came to a bed where things didn't seem quite

right. The patient was a man in his fifties, with a strong build. His beard was gun grey and densely cut like a hedge. He was looking at *The Economist*, which lay on his lap, but his hands were pushed down next to his hips, splinting his chest to make his breathing easier. His respiratory rate was elevated. He wasn't complaining, but his posture was.

Daniel filled me in. Mr Charles, fifty-six years old, admitted with sore throat the previous night. Past history of tonsillitis. Unable to eat and drink. IV antibiotics and steroids given. I asked him how he was feeling. 'Not so bad,' he said but even these few words made him a bit breathless. He wanted to keep his arms pressed down and his hands made quilty pits in the mattress. To talk to me he just lifted his eyes up, keeping his face down like coy girls do.

I took the notes and flicked through what had been written during the night. I found the script I was looking for. FNE: NAD. Flexible nasendoscopy: no abnormality discovered. Unsure of what to do next, I asked Daniel to fetch me the scope so I could have a look myself. This piece of equipment is about eighteen inches long. One end is an eyepiece, the rest is like a thin black snake made of fibre optics. The bendy bit is put inside the patient's nostril. The other end is held in the doctor's dominant hand. You hold it to your eye and look into the eyepiece. There is a little ridge on the top of this which your index finger can move up and down and this makes the snaky end move up and down inside the patient. You can look at all the dark crannies of the nose's interior. But you can also push it much further down and look at the vocal cords.

I passed the scope into Mr Charles's left nostril and entered the internal landscape of his nasal cavity. His septum lay on the left like a great straight wall, and on the right were his turbinates, like plush cushions in the corner of a dodgy nightclub. I negotiated the scope's tip over the inferior turbinate and under the middle one, noticing a rivulet of mucus coming from the entrance to the left maxillary sinus, as big as a waterfall. I went to the end of the nose, and then used the button on the eyepiece to make a ninety-degree downwards turn. Like a pot-holer, I advanced past the nasopharynx, a shady chamber flanked by the wonderfully named Caves of Rosenmuller, where nasal cancers sometimes hide. At this point, you usually come into the clearing of the hypopharynx and then see the larynx which looks like a teeny, tiny vagina.

On this occasion, though, I did not come into the customary clearing. I reached the nasopharynx but seemed unable to go further. I pulled the scope backwards just a little then tried to advance again. The same. In front of me was a wall of pink mucosa, swollen, cushiony, bright. I thought I must be banging into the adenoid or the posterior pharyngeal wall. Again, I tried and failed to make progress. Fleetingly, I wondered if my patient might be losing his airway. But this didn't make sense. If Mr Charles was in dire straits, it would surely be more obvious. Wouldn't he at least have stridor, that strained wheezy whistling you hear when someone is fighting to take in or let out breath through an obstructed airway? Wouldn't he be looking blue?

I felt instinctively that my patient was too well for this to be happening but also remembered something I had been told in my junior-doctor year that I had never since forgotten. Namely, if it crosses your mind that something

74

might be wrong with someone, do not ignore the thought. If what crossed your mind kills your patient, you will never forgive yourself or be forgiven.

These thoughts were in my mind, and my right eye was still up against the eyepiece, looking at Mr Charles's hypopharynx. In the two or three seconds it took me to ease the apparatus backwards and out of his nose, I had decided that I was going to have to call the registrar at home and ask him to come and have a look himself. So, when my view returned to the more general reality from the small significant geography it had been fixed on, I was surprised to see my suit on my legs, my briefcase by the bed, my SHO at my side, all of which reminded me of the obvious fact – amazingly forgotten – that the registrar on call that weekend was me.

As recently as the day before, if I had encountered a crisis of confidence about something, I would have shared it with the doctor standing next to me, my friend. But in this hyperaesthetic moment of discomfort, I felt that if I let the doubt that was in me out of my mouth and into the air, I would unravel. To buy myself a little thinking time, I said to the patient that I wanted to take the scope to a pot of sterilising fluid round the corner and then I'd come back and talk to him. I left the two men there and went into the sluice. I put the scope's long tail into a jug of sharp-smelling fluid and wrote the time on the piece of paper next to it so that whoever needed it next would know if it had soaked for long enough. Two different voices sounded in my head. One said: no one else was looking down that scope at that red realm but you. The examination last night was normal. The patient does not have stridor. He's probably fine. If you walk off the ward now, no one will know that you don't know what to make of what you saw. If the patient gets worse, you can always come back.

The other voice placed me back in the interviewing room where I had won my registrar number. I imagined myself being asked a question by one of the consultant interviewers. 'You are doing your first on-call as a specialist registrar. On the ward round, you see a man with a sore throat who does not show any overt signs of distress. But when you scope him, you cannot find any airway. What do you do?'

Immediately, I saw myself in my mind's eye, saying, 'This is an airway emergency. There is no time to lose.' And with that, I stepped back into the real world, like Mr Ben coming back from his dressing room into the shop. I returned to Mr Charles's bedside. I explained to him that, having looked down his throat, I was concerned that he might not be suffering from tonsillitis after all, but instead something more serious called supraglottitis. That I was concerned that if things became any worse, his throat might swell to the point where he wouldn't be able to breathe. I went on to say I wanted to take him to the operating theatre so that we could examine him under anaesthetic. We would probably put a tube down his throat and leave it there for twenty-four hours while we gave him medicine to reduce the infection and the swelling. I added that there was a chance he might wake up with a tube sticking out of his neck if we were unable to get one down his throat.

Mr Charles was laconic. Perhaps this was his nature. Or, perhaps this was just how a man who was about to suffocate would be. I used his muteness as an opportunity to call my consultant, who agreed to come in and stand by in the operating theatre in case an emergency tracheostomy was necessary. I also called the theatre nurse who put our case at the top of the weekend's emergency list. My junior colleague had succeeded in calling the anaesthetic registrar who was going to call his consultant in too, in case he found this airway a particularly difficult one to bypass.

By now, my private doubts were making me feel ill. I had perfomed an uncertain nasendoscopy. I wasn't sure at all that my patient was losing his airway. Maybe I had just examined him incompetently. There were two consultants on their way into the hospital during the weekend. Another doctor, the anaesthetic registrar, was probably waiting in theatre. Other emergency surgical cases would be postponed because of my hunch. There was no middle ground here, no spectrum of grey. Either the patient was completely fine, or his life was in immediate danger. If I was wrong to draw attention to this, my reputation would never recover. If I was right, I would have saved a life. Nowhere in this internal monologue was concern for the patient's welfare in evidence.

My sense of unease sharpened while I sat at theatre reception to wait for everybody to arrive. In front of me was the red ringbinder that held the day's emergency list. I opened it and looked down to see the last entry which was ours. Examination under anaesthetic airway. Plus or minus intubation. Plus or minus tracheostomy. Next to it was an arrow showing that our procedure should go before the one on the previous line. This line said 'Kidney Transplant'. As I read this, I felt the red folder I was holding open do a little jump on the beige grainy Formica counter and looked up to see that this had been caused by the banging down of a big square metal box which had a fluorescent pink label on the side, and that label said two things which were 'FRAGILE' and 'KIDNEY'.

Nothing could have made me feel more oppressed than this. Sitting next to this kidney on ice. A kidney that would have to wait to be plumbed into a needy abdomen because of what now felt like a whimsical doubt on my part about the patency of someone's airway. The next thing that happened was that everyone turned up at once. The patient, looking disconcertingly well on his trolley, led by a porter in his navy trousers and matching T-shirt. The two anaesthetic big-shots in their blues. My consultant, who breezily said, 'What's going on then?' as he wheeled an expensive black-framed bicycle into theatre reception. He was wearing an all-in-one cycling suit and had on his back one of those rucksacks that have a hidden tank and deliver water into the athlete's mouth via a tube. This tube was positioned near Mr Millard's mouth like a bizarre microphone. He was all excited from exercise and urgency. His activeness and readiness for more action made everything sink lower and lower inside me.

Like lambs to the slaughter, I thought grandly, the patient and I. He with his life on the line, me with my nascent reputation. We were soon in theatre. The anaesthetists were gassing Mr Charles down slowly while Mr Millard and I scrubbed and checked we had everything we needed on our trachy tray. I was grateful for the cover of my mask and gown for I had started to sweat and a blush of fear was rising and falling from my neck in sickening waves. Hot. Cool. Hot. Cool. As the anaesthetic registrar flicked open his laryngoscope with its curved metal tongue, and bent forwards over our supine charge, my only prayer was that Mr Charles should be in real trouble, about to die, even. Anything but OK. Let his airway be sick, I thought. Do not let that tube go down with ease. Please.

What usually happens is that the metal laryngoscope shows the anaesthetist where the cords are and then the rubber tube is guided along the edge of the scope and passes between these cords. And then a balloon is inflated which sits just below them in an area called the subglottis and anchors the tube in place. And then the other end of the tube, the one outside the patient's mouth, is attached to the oxygen tube.

But this anaesthetist took the laryngoscope out and repositioned it several times. He did not reach sideways for his consultant to lightly whack the tube into the palm of his hand. He heaved a bit. His Asian face had a reddish tinge to it. After a short while, during which time I hardly dared draw breath, he shook his head at his boss and stepped aside to let his senior have a go. I looked down at my gloved hands so that I didn't seem too keen to ask the anaesthetic reg exactly what he had seen. I held these hands in front of me in the manner of someone approving recently manicured nails, a buxom diamond engagement ring. I saw little drops of moisture within the web spaces of my fingers, on the other side of the waxy rubber.

The consultant anaesthetist had now been attempting to gain access to Mr Charles's airway for about a minute. My consultant was minutely shifting his weight from one foot to another, so that I intermittently felt the warmth of his right shoulder against my left one. Just as it was beginning to look inevitable that we would be performing our slash trachy, the consultant reached sideways. He had to flap his hand impatiently – his eyes still trained on the laryngoscope – because his junior had given up on the idea of handing the equipment to him. The breathing tube changed hands like a baton and was carried over the finish line. The consultant then stood back with satisfaction and turned to his registrar to say, 'Bastard of an airway, mate. Nearly couldn't get it in myself.'

Then he turned to Mr Millard and said, 'Rip-roaring supraglottitis. I'll let ITU know he's ours for a bit.' My consultant nodded, dumped his mask and gown in the black theatre bin and, with a nod to me, was gone. I stayed to clear up with the anaesthetic reg and then went off to finish the ward round. Some of the patients were antsy by now. They had been told by the staff nurse that their doctor would be round about eight. It was now eleven. But I didn't care. My suit felt stylish on me now, the thick handle of my leather briefcase warm and snug in the palm of my hand. Even Daniel seemed bouncier and less awkward about pushing the trolley for me than he had before. Imperceptibly, I had arrived.

Good surgeons are decisive. They don't hover over the operative field. This ability takes a certain courage, and is often accompanied by excessive self-confidence, never stronger than in youth. Although I did the right thing to take my patient to theatre that day, there is truth in the surgical saying that 'A good surgeon knows how to cut. A really good surgeon knows how not to.' Maybe one of the most important reasons we all train for so long is to ensure the self-doubt that is a part of getting older. This awareness of one's own limits may prove more life-saving than any knife.

TERRITORY

A doctor's first duty is to their patient. But success in a profession as competitive as surgery also requires a strong sense of self. Most of the time there is no conflict between these two things. But occasionally a tension arises between what is best for a patient and what is best for one's career. I have not always done the right thing under these circumstances.

Every morning during my first job in surgery, a departmental meeting was held to discuss what new patients had arrived overnight. We met in a seminar room which was arranged hierarchically, with four neatly arranged rows of seats. Consultants sat at the front, with their underlings in decreasing order of rank behind them. When everyone was assembled, the most junior member of the on-call team would stand at the front of the room and report on who they had admitted to hospital since the previous working day. It didn't take me long to notice that the junior surgeons most favoured by the consultants were those who brought in the fewest patients. And there were several occasions when I witnessed the public humiliation of a junior with an above average list of admissions.

Awareness of this petty human accounting influenced the way I behaved during one of my first on-calls. I was assisting in theatre when I was asked to go and see a lady with painful haemorrhoids in A&E. When I came off the phone and told my registrar where I was going, he chuckled. I interpreted his response as the disdain of a fully and excellently unfeeling surgeon, and concluded that piles were not enough to earn someone a position on an admissions list, or in a surgical bed.

So I suppose I had made my mind up about the fate of Gloria Mbele before I even met her. I took my keenness to emulate my registrar, the meanness of a child who wants to be friends with the school bully, into my consultation with her. As soon as I introduced myself to the middle-aged woman lying on the A&E cubicle couch, she told me what the problem was. She was a good historian, someone who tells you all the facts you want to know, in a coherent order, without excessive anecdotalising.

Mrs Mbele had suffered from haemorrhoids since the first of her four children was born. She had put up with mild symptoms for years but had never felt things were bad enough to mention to her doctor. That day, Mrs Mbele had done an extra shift in her cleaning job, to cover for a sick friend. She had noticed a feeling of increasing discomfort which she knew was coming from her piles, but had continued to work regardless, electing to finish what she was doing and then go straight home and have a bath.

In the privacy of her own house, she discovered that her piles had become as big as a plum. She was unable to push them back into her anus with a finger because they were so large and sore. So she had called her sister to come and stay and look after her children, and had taken the bus to A&E.

I wrote some brief notes on the clear story that Mrs Mbele had given me, and then excused myself briefly, to go and find some gloves and local anaesthetic jelly, to examine her. When I came back into the cubicle, she had already got herself into the right position. She was lying on her side, facing the wall. Her underwear was folded neatly on the hospital stool and she had put the pale blue perforated blanket over her bottom to protect her modesty, while she waited for me. Her position was a trusting one, and it touched me despite myself. And oddly, it made me think of that Rudyard Kipling poem about smuggling, with its line 'Watch the wall, my darling, while the gentlemen go by!'

I returned to the matter in hand. I explained to Mrs Mbele that I was going to have a look. I had reduced small haemorrhoids in clinic before, and hoped to be able to do the same thing here.

I lifted up the blanket and what I noticed first was that my patient had drawn her knees right up to her chest, unlike most people whose shyness means that they instinctively want to hide as much of their bottom as possible. In this case, the pain of anything touching her piles meant that Mrs Mbele was trying to make as much space for them as she could. Drawing her buttocks gently apart, I saw the haemorrhoids. Collectively the size of a peach, they were thrombosed and purple. If these venous abnormalities get stuck outside of the body, the tight muscular anal sphincter strangulates them. This causes them to swell and become extremely painful.

Just touching the tender mass caused Mrs Mbele to flinch, and I knew immediately that the kind thing to do would be to admit this poor woman onto the surgical ward, sit her on some ice overnight, prescribe her some strong analgesia and have another look at them the following day, by which time they would probably have shrunk significantly.

But my patient was not my only concern. I remembered all too clearly the disparaging expression on my registrar's face when I had mentioned someone attending A&E with a problem as trivial as piles. And I was thinking of the surgical meeting the next morning, and of how I would be mocked for bringing this lady in. I swiftly decided that I would not admit Gloria Mbele as an emergency if I could possibly avoid it.

This left me with the problem of finding a way to offer my patient some decent analgesia for the painful experience I was about to inflict on her. I replaced the blanket, and told her I would be back as soon as possible. I left A&E, and took the lift up to the labour ward. Once there, I managed to persuade one of the midwives to lend me a canister of Entonox, the gas cocktail of nitrous oxide and air used to placate women giving birth. Lugging this out of the lift, I returned to my patient's cubicle.

Tearing open several sachets of local anaesthetic, I lifted up Mrs Mbele's blanket, and coated her anal mass with

the jelly. It shone after this smearing and her haemorrhoids looked giant to me. I then passed Mrs Mbele the
Entonox mouthpiece. There was no need to explain to
her how to use it. She had had plenty of experience, she
said to me, with a brave, shaky sort of smile.

I braced myself and then took the exquisitely sensitive
swelling in the palm of my hand. My patient had the gas
and air tube in her mouth and I could tell from the whirring
noise it made that she was using it liberally. I had one
hand around her piles and the other was resting on her
shoulder which I hoped would be comforting although I
sensed her recoiling from me.

I could feel the mass of thrombosed tissue decompressing
in one hand just as I felt my patient's shaking body under
the other. Once the mass was more like the plum size she
had diffidently described to me earlier, I began to advance
my hand towards Mrs Mbele's anus. I was glad I had used
so much anaesthetic jelly, for I needed slipperiness on my
side to do what I had to, which was to return the
haemorrhoids back whence they came.

The piles were relatively small now and I sensed from
my patient's calmer breaths that her moment of extreme
pain had passed. Using my index and middle fingers as
a splint, I pushed the slackened tissue into Mrs Mbele's
anus. I then sat down, half of my hand still warm inside
her, to wait for the haemorrhoids to completely shrink
away. The last thing I wanted was for them to slip back
out, for the process of venous engorgement to start again.
I looked down at my blues-clad knee and saw it was
trembling.

After five minutes in this position, I withdrew from my
patient and covered her up again. Despite nominal success,

I was uncomfortable, a sensation which I only recognised much later as shame. But in that moment, I shrugged off the unpleasant feeling, and congratulated myself for enabling Mrs Mbele to return home to her children. I explained that her haemarrhoids were reduced, at least for now. I gave her a box of lignocaine jelly sachets, which I said she could apply to her back passage after bathing. I then made her an outpatient's appointment with the general surgeons. I thought there was a good chance she would need a haemorrhoidectomy at a later date.

There was no need to admit anyone else that night. My list of patients remained within the neat confines of one A4 page, and at the surgical handover meeting the following morning I sensed the consultants were pleased with me. Mrs Mbele's name persisted only in my mind, her pain a lacuna, an unrecognised event that I hoped had improved my surgical standing.

That event with Gloria Mbele was by no means isolated. Within a couple of months, I was hotly in the swing of gaining a reputation for myself as a no-nonsense young surgeon who didn't make unnecessary work for her bosses, who didn't create long ward rounds, who didn't display that worst of faults, sentiment. It took a completely random event which occurred to me when I wasn't at work to make me realise the error of my territorial perspective.

I had been on holiday for a week in America and had just taken the red-eye flight back to London. The plane had landed early at Heathrow. I was walking through the terminal, and as I passed from one electrical walkway onto the few metres of carpet that separated it from the next one, the right inferior quadrant of my visual field was filled with the sight of a man lying on his back on the ground. Next to him was a suitcase, and together they formed a monochrome island in the patterned surrounds of the airport carpet. I actually noticed the suitcase before I noticed him, because I suppose luggage is what you expect to see at ground level in airports.

I noticed the suitcase and the man as I was striding, and because the piece of still ground between the two moving strips was short, I crossed it quickly. It was only when my foot touched down on the second walkway, that part of my brain registered that what mattered in this visual grouping, was not the suitcase but the man. Because he was completely still and blue.

However, my observation was slower and more clouded than what was happening to the rest of me. My feet were on the straight, deep-grooved rubber matting of the conveyor belt. The hand not carrying my bag was stretched around the wide rubber handrail. The momentum of the belt was carrying me away from where my eye had been and where my mind's eye remained.

By the time I fully recognised that I had just seen a dead man lying on the ground by himself in Terminal Four of Heathrow airport, I was physically a long way from him, fifteen metres or so, without actually having taken a single step. I had not walked away, but it was as if I had, as if all the times I had walked away from people meant that I no longer even needed to move my feet to be absent, as if the historical fact of my tendency to bolt was enough to ensure cowardly distance-making wherever I went.

I turned around and ran back the wrong way along the travelling mat. It would have been easier to wait until I had got to the end of my short rubber journey, and then go back along stationary ground. But I suddenly needed to feel that I was not being carried away from the scene my brain had now registered. I wanted to know that, for once, I was a doctor running towards someone's need.

I only had to push past a few people, and soon I was back between the two conveyors, and I had put my bag next to the suitcase which was beside the man whose motionlessness seemed a sort of patient waiting, a new chance. At close quarters, he looked unequivocally dead. I checked his airway and could find nothing blocking it. I also looked and listened for any breath and felt for a pulse. There were no signs of life. I didn't know how long this man had been lying there, but there was a certain solidity to his inertia, to the thickness of the air moulded around him, that made me suspect he had not been alive for some time.

The only thing for it was to start CPR. Suppressing my distaste at the prospect of this lifeless kiss, I embarked on the algorithm of mouth-to-mouth and chest compressions, a medical score known by all doctors. Nothing I did made any difference. The only change I noticed was someone putting a screen around me and my charge. It was a boudoir sort of thing, something that you might expect to see bras and knickers flying out from the back of.

This had been done by a young airport official, and he had also brought me an automatic heart-shocking machine, called an Annie defibrillator. This can be used by anyone on someone who has had a cardiac arrest. It reads a patient's heart rhythm via sensors attached to the chest, and a voice tells you when to shock the patient, which you do by simply pressing a button.

The airport official rigged the machine up to the patient's

chest, then turned to me. I felt fraudulent at the way this helpful young man looked at me, with awe in his eyes, when I told him I was a doctor. I knew by this stage that I had arrived too late to do anything genuinely useful.

I followed the directions given by the machine's electronic voice, delivering a series of fruitless shocks to the stranger's chest, until some paramedics arrived a few minutes later. Then the airport official packed up the machine, and the ambulance men packed up the corpse. I picked up my bag and stepped out from behind the screen to join the other passengers passing from one conveyor belt to another. The few that saw me eyed me inquisitively, but within a couple of track-travelled metres, I lost my separateness and became just like everyone else.

Just before I reached the end of the conveyor belt that I had stepped onto for the second time that morning, the young airport official, out of breath from running to catch me, tapped my shoulder. He had been sent by his senior to get my name and address, presumably for their records. I already felt that I had moved on so his exclamation that 'I saw him as they put him in the ambulance and I'm sure I saw him move. I think you saved his life,' seemed as incongruous as it was unlikely.

Three days later, I received a letter of thanks from the airport, and a free return flight to anywhere in the world. A generous reward for doing so little. I used this ticket for a lovely holiday in the West Indies, but always felt it was more than I had deserved. That I had only responded as I was meant to. As I had often not done in the past.

At the graduation ceremony that marked the transition of the whole of my year from medical students into doctors, we were addressed by the Dean about the duties of the profession we were entering. I remember him saying that the greatest privilege our job conferred was that of looking after people in their most vulnerable moments. And I also recall thinking that the point he made was rather an obvious one.

But it was not obvious. In my first couple of years of surgical training, I often put myself before my patients. Either because I thought I would get ahead in my career by doing so, or just because I was afraid I would look like a wimp if I didn't. That day in the airport, when I went to help and found I couldn't, I thought back to my graduation talk and realised I had forgotten its main message. That more fundamental than being a surgeon is being a doctor. And that the single most important part of the job is protecting the interests of those you are lucky enough to be looking after.

EMERGENCIES

Perhaps the most exciting six months in any junior doctor's training are those spent in A&E. Nothing is gentle there. Catastrophes abound, the diseases are dire, the episodes of human dislocation momentous. But what struck me most about this department during my first few days working there was that all visitors to A&E seemed to be coming there to lose something. Some were losing a loved one, some their own life. There were suicide attempts by people who had lost faith. There were incidents that caused loss of limb. There were unforeseen events that caused loss of function or loss of beauty. There were illnesses that were severe enough to result in loss of personality. I came to see A&E as a sort of departure lounge in which every patient had come to say goodbye to someone or something, often with no warning, usually with no time or peace or preparation.

Within this pageant of loss, I remember the quiet case of Cheyenne. Her casualty card, picked from the top of a stack which never dwindled, said bleeding per vaginum, cubicle three. I found her looking forlorn in this six foot by four foot space, which was separated from the menagerie of the rest of the department only by some thin partitioning and a curtain. She wore a hospital gown, which had the name of the hospital written across it diagonally in a small font over and over again, alternately in yellow and brown, like punishment lines from school. She was wearing a lot of make-up and I thought how old I was compared to her. Her hair was a bad blonde and she had big hoop earrings in her ears, but she had obviously given up on her efforts at foot level, because they were grimy and her toenails uncut and grey.

I said a matey sort of 'Hi', hoping this would put me on her level. Then I collected some blood by putting a cannula in a vein in her arm, in case she needed a transfusion. I connected a drip to this same tube and started up some IV fluids. Finally, I settled down to hear her story.

My patient was sixteen years old and twelve weeks pregnant. The pregnancy had been unplanned but was not unwelcome, except for Cheyenne's mother who was so angry that she had thrown her daughter out of the house. Cheyenne had been staying with her boyfriend's parents for the past few weeks. The bleeding had started that afternoon during her shift at the supermarket. In the past hour she had changed her sanitary towel five times.

She was alone as she told me her story. She said her boyfriend was going to come when he finished work. She was calm to begin with, but soon became uncomfortable and then complained of severe pelvic pain. I told her I needed to have a look. I put on my gloves and tried to shield the tray of instruments I had brought in with me with my body. I unwrapped the gynae pack from the green sterile paper which made it looked like a merry present. Everything inside the metal tray appeared unkind, and at its base was a platform with holes in it so that any blood could trickle through it and collect below and not swamp the useful tools.

She lay back and I positioned the anglepoise lamp, which was attached to the wall, so that its wedge of light entered her. She had let her knees fall apart with her feet still together without my direction, and something about this made me feel sad. I pushed an inco-pad, like a baby's disposable changing-mat, under the W of her bottom. At first, all I could see was blood flowing from her. I was near enough that I could see the tiny particles in it moving out and onto the white pad.

Telling this stoical bleeding girl what I was doing, I put a shiny bullet-shaped metal speculum inside her vagina and spun its metal screw so that the two curved sides of it winched her open. Blood was pouring from her and I decided that if things went on like this for much longer, I would have to move her round to Resus, where you put people if you think they might die. But I had something to do first, that I hoped would help.

What I wanted to check was her os. This is the mouth of the cervix. The door which leads from the accessible vagina into the less accessible uterus. When someone is having a miscarriage, this can get held open by a clot of blood which in turn causes extra bleeding and pain. I had been taught that clearing the os can improve things.

Cheyenne's whole body was shaking and she was crying. Directing the light further inside her, I could see that the os was indeed being held open by a piece of tissue, a bit of what is medically known by that coldest of words, 'product'. I reached for the longest set of forceps in the pack. I regretted the steely clattering noise I made as I dislodged this instrument from the other things that lay there. These forceps sit in your thumb and finger like scissors. And then the long arms curve out and then back together in two little circles which meet in a clasp.

I told Cheyenne that I was going to try and stop her pain and her bleeding and I reached inside her. I apposed thumb and fingers so that the forceps came together in a decent grasp around the stuff that was sticking out of her womb. I pulled, expecting this clump to come away and for the os to close. Instead, Cheyenne made a pushing noise and an action to go with it, and a dark mass the size of a grapefruit emerged from her os, travelled the short length of her vagina and emptied itself on the inco-pad.

I was aghast. I felt sick and alarmed and didn't know what to do. Cheyenne's head was thrown back with physical relief and I was glad that she couldn't see my face, which would not have looked good. I glanced down. In the pool of blood that was making an ever bigger circle in the quilted white pad, I saw the shape of a baby. Head, arms, legs, back. All curled up.

Automatically, I folded the top of the inco-pad softly over this mass and, still holding the bloody tongs, I stepped back the two paces it took me to get to the curtain. I didn't want to turn my back on Cheyenne's face, because I didn't want her to see what I had seen. I put my head round the curtain, tucking its rough material under my chin, so that just my face poked out. I really wanted a nurse. Two of my doctor friends were writing notes at the central station a metre or so from where I stood. I remember thinking how strange A&E was, with its distinct bloody universes, all rammed up next to each other. One of them looked alarmed at the sight of me and said, 'What do you need?' 'Nurse,' I said, and pulled my head back inside.

In the few seconds that my eyes had left Cheyenne, she had sat forwards. Her legs were still apart, as before. She had folded back the leaf of the inco-pad. There was blood everywhere, but she seemed not to notice or mind. Her face was dry and looked unbelievably sweet. With one finger she was touching the gory mass in front of her ever so gently and she turned her young glance to me and said, 'My baby.'

Then a nurse arrived with a tray into which she carefully lifted the inco-pad with its contents. Behind her was the duty gynaecologist, whom one of my colleagues must have called on my behalf. He said, 'I'll take over from here.' And then Cheyenne's boyfriend was there, and their teenage faces disappeared within their closed hug, and I knew that the opportunity for me to say anything meaningful to her had passed. I left the cubicle, to change my scrubs, to see the next patient. I have always wondered how those remains were disposed of.

Ten to fifteen such dramas played themselves out in the average twelve-hour shift in A&E. But however constant the flow of work, these desperate cases seemed un-connected. People either went home, or died, or were taken off to another area in the hospital to receive definitive care under other doctors, who would come to understand how the first shocking event that had brought them into the department fitted into some wider context.

For me, these patients seemed assorted into the random packages of my days, of cycle rides taking me to and from work, of changes out of dirty scrubs and into clean ones. I began to feel demoralised. Emptied. Cast down by all the loss and the viciousness. The drunken horrors, the strip-lit awfulness of life gone wrong. And all of this was playing itself out against the blankening canvas of my own life.

As doctors, the shift system of A&E had wrenched us from normal daily patterns, making any life outside of medicine hard. Our weekends and evenings were rarely our own; our days off tended to happen when everyone else we knew was at work. We shared amongst ourselves this sense of suspension in our lives. Relationships with people outside work fell apart and were replaced by new temporary ones within our close group.

Dislocation seemed all around, including on a much more significant, world scale. In New York, the twin towers were attacked and in the relatively unimportant locus of our A&E, we observed a unique phenomenon in the department's history: all the patients went home. We doctors sat in the empty waiting room watching the events unfold on television, in London's busiest emergency unit, nobody for us to treat.

Perhaps all of this gave rise to a need to recast the scene into something more optimistic. Because around halfway through my time in A&E, I stopped noticing all the loss and the doom. I started to pay more attention to whatever I could find amongst the chaos that might redeem it. I began to notice frills of kindness in the violent scenes, shreds of goodness that persisted through the bad. The modestly successful outcomes that laced the tide of hopeless ones. I forcibly observed, amongst all the disaster, a human heart drive towards some sort of community, to reconciliation, to harbour.

In what had previously seemed an inchoate workaday life, patterns emerged. There were patterns of clinical presentation, cases that echoed other cases, already seen. The fractured neck of femur in an old lady, the young man with ureteric colic. The rectal bleeds and bloody drunks. The feverish kids and rude grown-ups. There was also the constant of my own role in the department, although this was perhaps only tenuously reassuring. I remember asking one of the most experienced A&E nurses one day, with a sorry tone in my voice, 'Am I going to get called a cunt every single day in this job?' To which she replied, 'Just be grateful you're not being called a fat cunt.'

As a group of doctors, we had also formed a close group by this stage, with the usual characters and kinship dynamics. And just as the department provided us with a sense of community, so I noticed that A&E was home to many of the local unemployed. The waiting room was comfortable, with a new carpet, comfy chairs and a plasma screen TV. Every day, a group of men would congregate there, posing as patients, especially if there was some major sporting event on TV. They found the best seats and tucked their beer-packed holdalls under them. I even saw someone nipping into majors one evening at exactly the right time for the catering trolley, and returning to his station in front of the telly, hot meal on lap, and can of beer soldiered behind the leg of his chair.

These guys had a sense of belonging there; it was their

spot. I saw them every evening that I arrived in or left the hospital. I'd push my bicycle through the waiting room and there they'd be. One evening, I was doing just this, going home helmet and anorak already on. Day-Glo stripes at ankle and chest. Suddenly, one of the punters had blocked me by standing in front of my bike. He had the front wheel trapped between his legs and the handlebars in his hands and he faced me, so that I saw the pores in his face, and said, 'Where do you think you're going, Doctor?' I don't think he meant this as a joke. Perhaps it was just too much to contemplate that any of us had somewhere else to go.

Mostly, though, I noticed a desire or drive for community within the patients' individual cases. In my mind's eye, I see a row of A&E cubicles like rooms in a doll's house in which good and order strained against disaster and accident. Knife-attack boys who came in having slashed each other, but left as friends. Deliberate self-harmers who came for regular conversation, as well as to have their cuts sutured. Families realising they loved each other, if only briefly, when death came knocking. And other, more mixed images like these.

I was sitting at the central station writing notes on a patient. I was near the CCTV screen, which showed what was going on inside the locked psychiatric room, a place with a proper door set aside for any patient deemed to be in a hazardous phase of a mental illness. I could see a black woman crouching in one corner at the bottom left-hand side of the TV. She was in the position of someone about to do a dive-bomb into a swimming pool, arms clasped round scrunched knees, head on arms.

I couldn't see John, my doctor friend, who was also in the room trying to find out why she had been found balled up like this in a supermarket aisle, refusing to speak or move. But I could hear his Northern voice talking to her, trying to coax something out of her. I was looking by turns down at my notes, up from my notes, sideways to the black-and-white TV screen when I was trying to fix a thought, down to my notes to write. Then the woman bounded up and I saw the back of John's head enter the screen like a big blur in the foreground. He had taken a step forward and his arms were held out slightly. Whether from a startled reflex of self-protection or in a desire to comfort, I couldn't tell.

The next thing was that she was pulling off her jumper. Then awkwardly pulling off her trousers, which were tight around the ankles and caught on her shoes so that she had to use one hand to support herself against the wall. I could see the dangling middle part of her wobbling with the effort of pulling at her shoes to get them off so that the trousers could follow. After this little undressing hitch, it was no time before all her clothes were off. And then there was a naked woman on the screen advancing into the camera view although of course not approaching the camera so much as approaching the space where I knew John stood. I could hear her voice now in little gravelly bursts, masculine almost in its urgency, saying first quietly, 'Fuck me,' over and over again, and then more loudly, and emphasising the pronoun of her lost self, 'Fuck *me*, Doctor, fuck *me*, fuck *me*, fuck *me*!'

The part of John's head that had briefly entered my view was not visible now, and I guessed he had taken a step back again, and perhaps was doing his best to press himself into the unyielding wall behind him. I started at the feel of breath behind me, and turned to see one of the male nurses reaching under my legs to get a blue hospital blanket out of a cupboard there. He crossed to the psych room and left the real world in front of me, to reappear a second later in the black-and-white hinterland of the TV screen, where he advanced certainly on the disintegrating woman, whose most basic urge, whatever her loss, was for company, for human communion, for expiation of disaster in the warmth of someone's arms. The rough blanket was soft about her and the door opened again to let John escape.

The persistence of human need for human, I also witnessed in the first assault victim I ever saw. I remember the cubicle I treated her in. This A&E department owned a funny old medical light, which looked like the kind of apparatus you might find on a film set. It was an upright structure with a big black tilting sunflower head that could be turned this way or that to cast its humming glare on any situation warranting white scrutiny. The way this vast head moved was disconcertingly human, a graceful face on a toned neck.

Someone had put this light in the cubicle with the patient I was about to see, perhaps to make up for the fact that it was one of those budget cubicles with no bed in it. When I went in, I was struck by the oddness of seeing a young woman sitting on a stool, and the nosy black light trained on her face. Its shine struck her so brightly that I couldn't even see the colour of her hair, which glowed spun silver, or her skin. And her pose was so still. But what I could see in this silent still-life glare – which she somehow couldn't resist the drama of, because her posture was light and straight and she was allowing the gaze of this light to dote on her uninterrupted and with no coyness – what I could see brightly was the imprint of a shoe across her face. That someone had stamped on her face.

I don't know how something that had made such a mark could have left the underlying face so relatively unharmed. This lady did not seem distressed and was not interested in conversation. She was monosyllabic. She did not want to tell the story, which emerged despite her, which was that she had annoyed her boyfriend so he had pushed her over and stamped his boot on her face.

I have a triptych of impressions from this. The way she looked when I found her. The feeling of cleaning her face with sterile swabs to make sure the grit from the shoe wasn't on it. As I did this, I was looking at the tread marks on her face. I was marvelling at their distinct neatness. As I drew a swab across them, I could feel the way the swab recognised the dints of the depressed treads against the raised untouched interstices. For some reason, it made my head full of that noise that you hear when you drive over a cattle grid. Sort of takatakataka.

Then my third snapshot is of when her boyfriend arrived and tears of relief filled her eyes and they embraced. His pose was that of the generous indulger, whereas she was demure. And he was saying, 'Sorry, babe, sorry.' And she was saying, 'I'm sorry too,' and it seemed a joke between them that I offered her social services support. A joke which they found so funny that they were still laughing about it even as they left the department together, holding hands back into their life.

*   *   *

Gabriel Weston

These two women, the psychiatric patient and the assault victim, are hardly romantic heroines. And truthfully, their impulses towards human comfort might seem pathetic. I wonder now whether my insistence on noticing such things during my stint in A&E had more to do with my need to see things in a way that allowed me to keep doing my job, than anything particularly heart-warming about what I experienced of human nature in that most extreme of environments, the emergency department.

AMBITION

Once you have seen the bloom of a decent surgical incision, nothing in nature looks bright by comparison. This is my thought as I sit down to a breakfast of soft-yolked eggs, kidneys, bacon and toast. A carnal meal for an arguably venal day, whose list is set aside for one case only: hemiglossectomy, neck dissection and reconstruction with radial forearm flap. I am excited about this task with its promise of the surgical ideals of drama, danger and cure. But I am also uneasy. I can't shake off the feeling that there is something indecent about my high spirits, that I have not been entirely straight with my patient.

I first met Mrs Macnamara in a routine head and neck cancer follow-up clinic. A pre-consultation skim through the notes revealed: she is a heavy smoker, loves Tennent's B, is a recent survivor of a right tonsil cancer for which her treatment – chemoradiotherapy – was completed three years back. Subsequent follow-up has been regular but reluctant. Clinic letters do not refer to 'this lovely lady'; doctors seem miffed. Between references to this or that clinical feature rings a chorus of hectoring about smoking and drinking.

I am prepared for a rough, tricky woman, someone who will dislike what I represent, a patient I will have to suck up to. I hear the nurse calling Mrs Macnamara's name and, shortly after, soft steps in the corridor. The person who comes to sit opposite me seems shy and smiles. She is in her fifties but looks puerile in an outsize man's football shirt, has sloping shoulders and an ample middle. Her face is curiously uninjured by adult expression. There is something of Mrs Tiggy-Winkle about her.

The consultation proceeds as it should, a sort of individuated template in which specific human interaction seasons a series of points that must be covered. Eating, swallowing, speech all OK – no local recurrence. Lump-free neck – no apparent regional spread. Otherwise well – no suggestion of secondary cancer. Spare with words, Mrs Macnamara is nonetheless helpful and pleasant throughout. It is not until I have put my headlight on and am beginning the head and neck examination, starting with the oral cavity and oropharynx, that my patient palpably flinches. I have put my metal speculum on a large ulcerating lesion involving the right aspect of her tongue.

'Is that sore?' I ask, not needing confirmation of the obvious, but rather wanting her to tell me something about this excavated area in her mouth. 'Oh, that little blister.' Her words are blithe but the voice that breathes them strained. Her face is pink and damp now and she has developed a fine tremor. 'Oh, I don't trouble about that.'

The denial is valiant and touches me. Given how uncomfortable the smallest of benign ulcers can be, I know that the cancer now colonising this woman's mouth must be unbearably painful.

But alongside this sense of empathy jostle other heartier emotions: excitement, anticipation, something like a miniature version of pride. New to the specialty of head and neck surgery, I still feel callow and unconfident of my skills. I regularly find it difficult to assert my right to 'cutting' when there are other surgeons competing for experience. So to know that I have made a diagnosis, that my anxious eyes have detected a sneaky cancer that would otherwise have eluded notice, gives me a little kick. My boss will be impressed, and pleasing him is my surest path to surgical action.

The head and neck surgery department is set up to support moments of tumour discovery. Paper protocols piled neatly nearby outline what should happen next: biopsy, MRI scan, discussion, treatment. Blank pages in a secretary's surgical calendar await the imprint of Mrs Macnamara's name; a hulking scanner metres away from where we sit is ready to decipher and depict the extent of her disease; medical and surgical consultants swarm with vying therapeutic heroics. All that is required of me is to lead my patient through this ordained process. After a brief conversation with my consultant, who confirms my hope that the position of this tumour makes it amenable to surgery, I explain to Mrs Macnamara that we will need to take X-rays and a biopsy from her tongue under general anaesthetic. And although her nod signals acknowledgement, it also seems to shake us out of our previously friendly communion, so that we now feel on different trajectories. It is an uncomfortable dislocation but I defer thinking about it any further until we have a definite diagnosis.

This happens a week later, during which time our patient has had her biopsy. I am called into my consultant's room to provide a familiar face while he confirms to Mrs Macnamara that she has recurrent cancer. He is a kind surgeon but a bombastic one; I do not think that it occurs to him that his offer of the knife could conceivably provoke fear; I do not think he observes the glassiness in this woman's eyes as she impassively bows before his bad news and his great presence.

He outlines the bare bones of what will happen to her: there is cancer, it must be removed. It is a felicitous day because the prospect of cure is clear. A reconstructive consultant is called in and he too is optimistic: taking out the cancer will not leave a horrible hole since she still has a resourceful and wondrous body which can donate flesh from one site to another. These men are quickened by the prospect of an enjoyable operation and it makes their mood bountiful. Mrs Macnamara keeps looking at me, and if ever I have been looked at with appeal, it is now. I feel that she is asking me to arrest the whole unfolding scene, to intervene, to offer something smaller and softer by way of remedy. I think she wants me to tell these potentates to leave her alone.

I don't. I am a new registrar and a woman. I want my seniors to see me as one of their own, to observe my crisp unsentimental nature. I have vague recollections of a chapter in some textbook I have read recently, which sets out the minimum requirements for a patient's informed consent: time to consider the diagnosis, a menu of alternative solutions, a clear delineation of surgical risk, the opportunity to talk things over with a relative, friend or nurse. In cancer management, there is not the luxury of time, but this is a thin defence against my mute but growing sense that this lady's feelings and thoughts are receiving no consideration at all.

Within a minute, she has signed the consent form and agreed to come in for major surgery in four days' time. Although she knows that the cancer will not go away on its own, she has not been given an option as to what happens next. Her understanding of the approaching surgery is flimsy. She has not been told about how things will be when she wakes up, that there will be pain, that talking and eating may be difficult, that she will have a long hospital stay, that there is the possibility she may die in theatre. Her psychological preparedness for the bizarreness of reconstructive surgery has not been broached. I say nothing and return to my room to see other patients.

A few days later, I am approached by an unhappy-looking boss. He hands me a slip of paper with a phone number on it and mutters something about how our patient has refused to come into hospital the following day. Annoyed that his list has been disrupted at this late stage, he asks me to try and bring her round.

When I call Mrs Macnamara's house, her husband answers the phone. He is gruff. I introduce myself in a trilling, doctorish voice that I can hear sounds irritating. 'She doesn't want to talk to you,' he replies plainly. I sense this man finds my tone insufferable and am grateful that he passes the phone to his wife instead of hanging up. Softly, she says, 'Hello.' In a lame attempt to draw her to me, I introduce myself by my first name and then wheedle, 'I understand from the nurses that you don't want to come into hospital. Pehaps you could tell me what is troubling you so that I can reassure you.' 'Oh, I think I'm better off at home. That little blister really doesn't bother me, you know.' Her comment is as unbelievable as it is stoical.

I really want this woman to come into hospital. I don't want to declare defeat to my boss, whose view of me will strongly influence my surgical future. I don't want to miss out on the opportunity to assist in an exciting operation. And, since I am absolutely persuaded by a grounding in surgical pathology which tells me that this lady can be cured, I cannot bear the idea that she might suffer a horrible, painful end to her life because of my powerlessness to persuade.

Keen on conquest, I become downright phony: 'Kate, having met you in clinic, I know what an intelligent woman you are.' The ensuing pause encourages me in my seduction. 'I know that you are afraid you have cancer again, and I won't lie to you: we are worried about that too. The wonderful thing is that if you let us help you, we can make it go away. Whereas, without our help, it may kill you.' I am amazed at the effect of my proselytising for with a simple 'All right,' Mrs Macnamara agrees to come in.

The day of Mrs Macnamara's operation arrives and my uneasiness is eclipsed by excitement. Theatre today is a performance in three acts: neck dissection, or removal of all the cancerous lymph nodes from one side of the neck; hemiglossectomy, which means taking out half of the tongue with its associated cancer, and finally reconstruction, which involves using a piece of muscle from the forearm to fill the hole where the tumour once was. The operation will take most of the day. My own role is likely to be ancillary: holding retractors to give my consultants a good view, cauterising small bleeding vessels with a little soldering iron, known as diathermy, sewing up the wound at the end if I am lucky. I have been training for eleven years but am accustomed to the painstakingly slow acquisition of operative experience; the joke goes that the hard-earned MRCS does not only denote Member of the Royal College of Surgeons but – more aptly – Maybe Ready to Close Skin.

There is a likeness between preparation for a dinner party and an operation. In one, the careful arrangement of tablecloth, place settings, candles and ornaments seems an expression of necessary social order within which conviviality can flourish. In theatre, the care taken in arranging the surgical field seems to presage the whole tone of the operation. And were more surgeons women or more men hosts, it would be observed that good surgeons lay a beautiful table.

Once anaesthetised, Mrs Macnamara is laid supine with a sandbag under her shoulders to optimise neck extension. The head is positioned away from the side of the neck that is to be cut open; she looks as if she is turning the other cheek. The area of skin to be operated on is painted carefully with Betadine-dipped swabs, held in forceps the size of barbecue tongs. A sterile drape is twisted around the head and upper face, which reminds me of a painting by Magritte. Other drapes mummify the body.

A steel nib and purple ink are used to describe the intended incision and a number of cross-hatches made across it with the back of the scalpel. These will serve as markers for reapposing the skin neatly when all is complete. Local anaesthetic and adrenaline, which constrict blood vessels and so minimise bleeding, are infiltrated into the skin and my boss asks for the number ten knife. For me, this moment just before surgery starts – when the scene is beautifully still and clean and just about to be neither – is perfectly exhilarating.

It is a point of surgical pride to achieve a swift and accurate first incision with one application of steel, and in the neck this should penetrate the skin and platysma, the muscle underlying it which makes our neck stretch when we grimace. Once this bloody line is drawn, it is rendered into three dimensions: brushstrokes with the blade lift skin and platysma off the underlying structures and these 'flaps' are raised on both sides. Within a few minutes, the marvellous anatomy of the neck flares into view, an amazing sight, undinted by repetition.

The neck dissection takes two hours and is a painstaking process of freeing yellow nodal clumps, like the pulp of fruit, from among vital and interwoven cables of varying calibre. Progress follows an order: level-one nodes sit in what is known as the submandibular triangle, under the jawbone. Levels two to four run sequentially along the steep camber of the internal jugular vein in thirds. Level five is in the posterior triangle, the dip above the collarbone. Each level has its dangers, some life-threatening like damage to major blood vessels, some only debilitating such as injury to nerves, many of which are finer than dental floss. These hazards give the operation its rhythm, its repeated gratifying cycles of suspense and relief.

Tumour removal comes next. I straighten the head and, in order to give optimum access to the mouth, a cut is made vertically downwards through the middle of the lower lip as far as the bottom of the chin. A saw which looks like a tiny, electrical pizza cutter is used to breach the underlying bone, so that the front of the lower face can be opened like a book. The tongue is transformed from something disappearing obscurely into a deep hole into the perfect operative canvas, mounted on its underlying musculature.

While I hold the front of the tongue forwards in a dry swab to stop it slipping, the walnut-sized tumour and surrounding tongue is removed with diathermy. This is a long metal wand heated by electricity to about 1,000 degrees centigrade which doubles up as knife and cauteriser, useful in an area with such a rich blood supply. The tissue here is dense, and as the tongue fasciculates under my fingers, the sharp emery tang of diathermy smoke pricks my nostrils.

Meantime, another surgeon is busy excising what is called a radial forearm flap. This is an area of skin and muscle taken from the belly of the lower arm and tailored to fit what will be the defect in the mouth. It is carefully measured out and crucially comes with an artery and vein. The forearm is the perfect site for this paddle, since a dual arterial supply to the hand means one vessel can usually be spared without any risk of gangrene. Within an hour, the lump of tissue with its dangling vessels is handed over and a bolt of skin – shaved with something resembling a large cheese cutter – is taken from the thigh and bandaged around the skinless area of arm.

The flap is positioned into the defect left by the tumour and excess corners are rounded with a pair of scissors. This feels like a really good episode of *Blue Peter*. And once the piebald cushion of the new tongue has been fashioned and sewn, vessels are fed into the neck. The radial artery is sewn into the superior thyroid artery which will now vitalise the flap, the radial vein into the external jugular vein.

We are at the denouement. Mrs Macnamara looks like a sleeping figure upon whom someone has rested several open red paperback books. All that remains to be done is the insertion of drains to prevent the accumulation of blood clots, and closure of tissue layers with stitches, screws and staples. The atmosphere in theatre changes. Someone has turned up the music, on this occasion Lemar, disappointingly seldom the elevated classical strains one is led to expect. Conversation has become jocose, although it is rarely overtly ribald any more. The operation has gone well. No death, no major blood loss, all important structures seemingly preserved. ITU awaits our patient. We've all been standing seven hours and I can't wait to get my mask off, have a drink and a pee.

Less than a week later, Mrs Macnamara is sitting up in bed, decorated by the drains and drips and catheters and paraphernalia of major surgery. Smiling, she seems framed and strangely important like a grotesquely enthroned queen. Her voice is muffled but comprehensible. She says she is well and looks it. Over the next week or so, the daily removal of tubes will punctuate her recovery. Physiotherapists will galvanise her into walking about. Speech therapists will help with her voice and with swallowing. Finally she will go home to her husband and, it is to be expected, her old habits.

In the meantime, the hospital pathologists have declared that all lymph nodes removed from Mrs Macnamara's neck are cancer-free. The last patient on the ward round, my boss is pleased to announce her cured. I am caught up in this surgical evangelism and feel inclined in retrospect to view my former fleeting discomfort about my patient's emotional welfare as meagre, even superstitious. She has had life-saving surgery; her cancer is gone; she is recovering well. So what that we did not put the world to rights together!

There is expediency in this. A clear boundary still exists between surgeon and patient, and I know which side of that line I need to stand on to do well. I am about to forget Mrs Macnamara. The ward round is over and a new list awaits me in theatre seven.

HELP

Doctors have received plenty of criticism for not knowing how to communicate. The brunt of the problem is felt by patients, who frequently think that their clinical care has been adversely affected by this deficiency. But there are also dangers associated with doctors not being able to communicate effectively with each other. Information can be misunderstood or lost. More crucially, perhaps, the chain of command which relies on junior doctors being able to seek advice from their seniors can break down. For these reasons, a lot of time is spent teaching qualified doctors how better to communicate. And no surgical training course seems complete now without time allocated to this task.

In a recent communication skills tutorial, I recall witnessing just how poor the interaction between two doctors can be. Miss Ngozi, one of my consultants, was teaching. We were ten surgical registrars, and we were halfway through an afternoon of role play. Each of us was to be given a scenario testing our ability to communicate properly.

The general standard of performance had been bad, and I was keen to have my turn before the intensity of peer ridicule rose any further. But there was still one person in front of me, Asim. This cocky young surgeon now rose to his feet, rolling his white linen sleeves up over his handsome brown arms as if he was about to spar. From a piece of paper in his hand, he read out the details of the scene he was to enact.

'You are the surgical registrar on call. You see a patient with acute mastoiditis who needs emergency surgery, and you do not feel equipped to perform it without senior supervision. Please call your consultant at home and ask him to come and assist you.'

One of the actors employed to help in the course stood up, but Miss Ngozi gestured for him to sit again, indicating that she would play this part. I wondered whether she too had been irked by the course's scripted assumption that the consultant would naturally be male.

With a perky little shake of her tailored shoulders, a pinky pursing of the lips, she got into role. And I was struck yet again by her beauty. Age cannot wither her, I thought, warming myself up for thespian action. She was wearing an impeccable little trouser suit and a lovely white blouse. By her feet sat a perfectly proportioned briefcase, like the receptacle in which Paddington Bear carries the marmalade sandwiches he cannot fit under his hat. It had sharp corners but its surface was the alluring hard-softness of a baby's forehead.

Returning to the scene in front of me, I saw that Asim had taken up his position at the centre of the circle of his viewing peers. But despite his confidence, he seemed uncertain of how to step into the world of make-believe. Miss Ngozi kept her seat, a boss at the end of a witching-hour phone line. And she started the skit off by trilling out the ring of an old-fashioned phone three times. She then lifted an imaginary receiver before saying 'Hello' in a sleepy voice. This set a few of us twitching nervously, it seemed such a private, such a bedroom tone.

In a lower, posher voice than his real one, Asim began, 'I am very sorry to disturb you, madam. This is Mr Choudry. I am the specialist registrar on call tonight.' Without waiting for a response, he began to describe the clinical situation written on the chit in front of him, adding extra details to give a fuller surgical picture. But what he did not do was ask for help.

I sensed Miss Ngozi's impatience. She started to tap her pointed shoe on the ground, and gave an ostentatiously huge, fanning yawn. I am sure she did this semi-humorously, but Asim's tone was irritated as he responded with, 'The fact of the matter is that I need to take this patient to theatre,' to which she immediately quipped, 'So, why don't you then? Are you saying that you can't do this yourself?'

'No,' he replied, drawing this word out. His head was tilted down, but his eyes sought Miss Ngozi's from under impressive brows. The arrangement of his lips and teeth looked more like a bite than a smile, as he said, 'I am in fact quite capable of doing this myself. I just wanted to inform you that this was my intention.'

Miss Ngozi had had enough. She tossed her clipboard

down onto one of the plastic chairs with what I expected would make a slapping sound, but in fact made a clatter. She started, and several of us jumped with her. Then, she sniffed pre-emptively and took the centre of the circle. With one of her slim arms, she gestured that she wanted Asim to resume his seat amongst the rest of us.

'Thank you, Asim.' She smiled at him directly, and approached him on soft quiet feet, no angle on her glance or her beauty. She went nearer still, and just as she came within a foot of a young man who no longer looked proud of himself, she returned to the middle of the circle. And then she pronounced, 'Asim may be the first junior registrar I have ever known who is capable of performing cortical mastoidectomy unassisted, but he is not the first to overestimate his own communication skills. What he missed was that this scenario was asking him to ask for help. It is critical that you all become proficient at knowing your limits. These aren't the dark ages in which I did my training. Ask your consultant for help and you will get it with no fight. OK. Who's next?'

Watching this scene unfold, I had been struck not just by the importance of learning how to ask for help directly – it hadn't just been Asim's failure to do this that seemed interesting; I had also observed that the words between these two had only made up a small part of their overall interaction. And this had reminded me of a time, not two months before, when I had asked a different consultant for help, and had also found a subtext to our conversation too.

On the night in question, I was on call from home and had been asked to come into the hospital by one of the junior doctors, to see a man who had swallowed a piece of glass. It is part of normal development for children to experiment with putting beads or bits of Lego into the nose or ears, or anywhere else they will fit. As I listened to the story from my bed I wondered if certain adults never evolve through this stage. Every medic I know has a list of bizarre foreign bodies they have removed from adult orifices. In my case, this includes a carrot and battery inserted into the rectum, a Bic biro pushed under the skin of the forearm and a boiled sweet, still in its wrapper, which one patient had lost inside her own vagina.

Arriving at the hospital I found my patient was unpleasant. Mr Smith was in majors, because of the sharp nature of what he had swallowed. He was a big fat sunburned man. He was sitting sideways on the bed, despite the attempts of a nurse to lie him back. His arms were held in what looked like a bodybuilding curve, slightly away from his torso, and his jaw had an pugnacious, almost prognathic set. A tattoo on one forearm, written in a bizarrely calligraphic font, read 'Hating'. And although the print was blurred, suggesting the body art had been there some time, the expression on Mr Smith's face showed the sentiment still had strong currency.

I introduced myself overbrightly, a gesture of optimism before receiving what I instinctively knew would be a rough response. My patient offered no name or hand-shake, merely stating, 'Took your bloody time, didn't you?' He then made a show of looking me up and down before letting his eyes rest intently on my ID badge. 'You are a doctor, aren't you?' was his gambit.

It is important not to become preoccupied by dislike for a patient, because doing so can mean you miss things. And I have found that the best way to handle people like

Mr Smith is to be extra polite to them, and absolutely correct. Nonetheless, I didn't want to acquiesce with so much as the word 'Yes' so I simply reintroduced myself again by name and position. I then added that I needed to make sure I had the important facts right. That he had swallowed a piece of glass and could feel it sticking in his throat.

Aggressively, and in short sentences, he told me his story. He had been in the pub. He had had a few, by which he meant ten pints. He had noticed an old rival on the other side of the room. When he went to take a leak, he had spat in the man's beer. When he came back from the loo, this other man had come around the bar with a beer bottle and smashed it against one of the walls in front of Mr Smith. The glass base of this smashed bottle had landed in Mr Smith's nearly empty pint glass of beer, with what my patient took to be an insulting splash. So Mr Smith had looked his foe in the eye, picked the glass up and downed it, ostentatiously swallowing the piece of glass with his last beery gulp. The other man had then retired to his seat, and Mr Smith had got a bus to hospital.

Examining my patient revealed little of note other than some mild tenderness when I pressed his thyroid cartilage. I stood behind him to palpate the rest of his neck and looked down on the childlike rolls of skin on the back of his shaven head. This part of him made him seem almost vulnerable, but I was reminded of his general animosity by the fact that I could see him holding his hands just above his lap, as if poised to grab an assailant. As if I myself might be seized at any moment if I examined him too thoroughly or crossed some undefined line. By talking

Mr Smith through each part of the brief examination as I reached it, I hoped to soften this threatening atmosphere.

What didn't show on examination was plain to see on the neck X-ray that my junior had organised. A circular piece of glass at the level of the thoracic oesophagus. Removing this obstruction would require a general anaesthetic and the passage of a rigid oesophagoscope into Mr Smith's gullet. I knew that this was a dangerous procedure and that I was not prepared to do it myself. The scope is rigid, the food pipe soft and easily torn. And a tear can be fatal.

As I was thinking these thoughts, I recognised the cardiothoracic registrar sitting a little way along the same bench, writing in a patient's notes. I knew he was much more experienced than me, so I thought I'd show him the X-ray, and tell him about my patient. As it happened, I was very glad I did because he pointed out that we would need a cardiothoracic team on hand in theatre while performing this oesophagoscopy. If the glass lacerated any major vessels as we were pulling it free, they would need to be there to do an open thoracotomy, and repair any life-threatening damage.

I was thinking what an idiot the patient was to have caused all this trouble. And also wondering how I was going to lure my consultant in from home to help. On call that night was Mr Graham, a fit and creepily handsome man in his fifties. A man with grey hair and a silver tongue. A foxy favourite with the secretaries. He had a reputation amongst the registrars for being incredibly hard to summon. An old-school surgeon, he had trained at a time when senior registrars were able to handle most surgical emergencies and was squarely unimpressed by how often

he was asked to come in. Rumour had it that he sometimes simply turned off his mobile phone.

As far as the task in hand was concerned, there was
no doubt I needed help. I had removed a 10p piece from
a child's throat under consultant supervision since
becoming a registrar, but otherwise had no experience of
handling the potentially hazardous oesophagoscope in an
emergency setting. I definitely needed Mr Graham alongside me if I was to free the glass from Mr Smith's insides.
With this in mind, I asked switchboard to call him and
was relieved when, after waiting out a few rings, he
answered. I began by introducing myself, and stated clearly
that I needed him to come in to help me in theatre. And
then I went back to the beginning of the history, to tell
him about Mr Smith.

But before I could get my story under way, Mr Graham
said, 'Oh, so I've got you tonight have I, Flossie?' I had
no idea why he had given me this vile diminutive, but
pressed on regardless, trying to ignore the luxurious
stretching-in-bed noises he was making all the while.

When I had finished, he said, 'Well, Flossie, I don't
know who's more annoying. Your Mr Smith, for being
such a tit, or you for waking me up.' I had been prepared
for a strict, impatient sort of response but not for this
horrible languor, this unseemly nicknaming. 'What am I
going to do with you?'

Keeping calm, I replied, 'Well, I would be very grateful
if you could come in and assist me. The cardiothoracics
consultant is already on his way.'

'Oh dear, dear. You know, I do like to give you boys
a bit of rope. Let you find your own way. It's the only
way you'll ever get anywhere, you know. But, if you're

telling me you're a damsel in distress . . . well, then you've seduced me. Is that what you're telling me, mmm?'

'Yes. I need your help, Mr Graham, I do,' I said, wanting at all cost to bring this conversation to an end.

'In that case, I'll come in and hold your hand,' he replied, just slightly less indolently. And the phone call was over, with no goodbyes. Leaving me feeling strangely compromised and sleazy.

He came and helped, and there was no question that he needed to be there. I wasn't able to pull the glass out, and had to hand over to Mr Graham, who succeeded without needing the cardiothoracics guys standing close by to wade in and save the day. And once he was in the hospital, surrounded by colleagues and drama, he even managed to communicate with me more normally.

But the universal surprise that was expressed by my registrar colleagues when I told them he had come to help reminded me of the nauseated feeling I had had when talking to Mr Graham on the phone. I sensed that our communication had not been straightforward or direct. I had asked for help as simply as I knew how, but still felt that I had been complicit in something else. That I had earned the rare gift of Mr Graham's assistance by an interaction that had had more than words in it.

And this was what I was reminded of that day in the communication skills tutorial when I had watched the way that Asim and Miss Ngozi had behaved with one another. The words they had spoken had only been a part of the text, because power and sex were somehow expressing themselves too, and getting in the way of clear and useful clinical discourse. I wondered whether there could ever be a situation in which help could be asked for simply and without complication. Wouldn't these obstacles fall away if two women were talking to each other? Surely I would encounter no such problems when asking for help from a female boss?

A couple of weeks after that course, I had the opportunity to find out. I was doing a pleasant general ENT list in theatre by myself. The anaesthetist was quick, the list had started on time and there had been no hitches. The grommets had gone in first time and all the patients had been children so their tonsils had popped out like little cherries, with no resistance. The last patient on the list was a large 25-year-old woman with a lifetime history of tonsillitis and quinsy. This is a complication of tonsillitis which causes pus to collect in the capsule that surrounds the tonsil. A simple tonsillectomy relies on the surgeon finding the plane between the tonsil and the muscle bed in which it lies. Quinsy often destroys this dissecting layer, and can make for a very tricky operation.

But what had given me cause for slight alarm about this lady when I had consented her was not her history of quinsy. No, it was the fact of her hair, which was that kind of auburn that leans right into being red. I found her sitting on her bed by the window looking out onto the garden, and the sunshine had found her head with its beam. I thought, beware of this coppery hair, this flame-coloured head. It is a common view among surgeons that redheads bleed profusely.

Superstitiously, I thought to myself, if I don't mention my thought to anyone else, she won't bleed. If I do, she will. And then the anaesthetist was there, and had pulled back the curtain to reveal me consenting her. And I met his eye and looked back at my patient just as a little cloud in the busy sky made room for the sun and there again was that thin ray of light coming right down on her head. I could see the glints of redness along each pretty keratinous shaft and I turned with a fatalistic smile to him and said, 'Hasn't she got lovely red hair?' And his look to me was the admonishing look one actor must give another before *Macbeth* when someone has said that word. Half-humorous, but also as if to say, now you've really done it.

The operation started well. I love tonsillectomy. And the advantage of an adult is their size, their very roominess. I had my headlight on, which looks like a potholing light, and I arranged the spot of it to the perfect size and brightness, using my hands as a template. I was in the usual position, sitting at the patient's head, upside down to her. I had draped all of her head above her mouth. Another drape covered her body. I had chosen the biggest metal gag, and had slotted it into the little winch whose job it is to keep the mouth open. Sometimes putting this in can be tricky. The anaesthetic tube has to be negotiated and the blade of the gag should fit right in the middle of the tongue, lifting that whole slippery muscle out of the way. But oftentimes, just as you are opening the gag, the tongue will slip to one side or another, forcing you to loosen the metal winch and start again.

This gag went in easily and I used the Draffin rods to steady it. These are two metal poles with holes in them. You cross them over in your hands like a wigwam so that two of the holes interlace. Then you hook the gag into these holes. It makes a kind of metal tent, holding the patient's mouth open. And here was my patient's oropharynx, perfectly exposed, tongue in the centre. Plenty of room for manoeuvre and two decent-sized tonsils. Big enough to grip onto. Small enough to leave me room to work. Two tonsil swabs lay gently through the holes of the rods like soft white fingers.

Using forceps in my left hand to hold the tonsil away from the muscle bed, I eyed the place where I would make my first cut and took the scissors the scrub nurse was offering me. This first cut tells all. If you can find the right plane with the first incision, the rest of the operation is usually straightforward. The end of the scissors' blades sliced through the capsule, revealing a clear little space between tonsil and constrictor muscle beneath it. I handed the instrument back and took the bipolar forceps, with which to proceed.

There is a view that if adult tonsils are easy to remove, the patient evidently hasn't had much tonsillitis and probably shouldn't be having the operation. Extracting this woman's right tonsil was just hard enough for me to feel that she had been appropriately listed. The tissue I was dissecting was fibrosed and had the texture of hardened chewing gum. There was enough blood coming from the operative field that I had to ask the scrub nurse to hold the sucker in a pool of blood around the area I was dissecting, which rose to keep pace with what she drained. But within this shiny pool, constant, changing, I could still see and feel that I was in the right place. And I knew from experience that the best thing I could do was remove the tonsil as quickly as possible, at which point the bleeding would slow down.

Within a short time, the right tonsil was attached by a thin pedicle at the tongue base. With one final squeeze of the diathermy, and a continued pulling of my left hand, the tonsil was out, leaving a wet fossa in its wake. I picked up one of the slim swabs in some forceps and laid it along the length of this canal, doubling it over at the superior pole and then back again, so that the oozing bed had gauze tucked into it, like a snug eiderdown.

Things were going well and, with a satisfied sigh, I reached for the Luc's forceps again to do the other side, to perform the mirror-image operation. It is an idiosyncrasy of ENT surgery that you have to learn to operate ambidextrously, there are so many paired organs requiring attention. I was aware as I started this second half of the operation that the left was the quinsy side, and that it might be harder than the side I had already done.

Retracting the tonsil out of its fossa with my forceps, I eyed the part of the overlying mucosa where I wanted to make my first, short cut. I took the scissors from the scrub nurse, offered and received vertically in the curious tonsillectomy mode that means you use the butt of the blades to cut, not their length. I made my incision and tried to sneak one of the scissor blades up and under the capsule that I had cut, to see where I should begin dissecting with the bipolar diathermy. I found the mucosa totally adherent and fibrosed to the underlying tissue.

I sensed this was going to be a typical, horrible quinsy tonsil, but nonetheless made an attempt with the bipolar diathermy forceps to find a plane in which to proceed. All this did was start some hearty bleeding. I had done my best to make my first cut near the tonsil, so as not to disrupt the normal architecture of the anterior faucal pillar. But now, instead of peeling the tonsil off its bed, I found that I had entered the lumpy, pulpy substance of the gland itself. Blood was pouring out from the tonsil and every time I tried to grab onto the meat of it, bits broke off and the whole thing bled more and more.

I tried to go back to where I had started, to find another point of entry. It's a bit like when you peel a hard-boiled egg. Sometimes the shell skirts off the slippery white underneath in one go. At other times, as you pick the shell off, it sticks and lumps of white come with it and the whole thing is a miserable mess. Anyway, I couldn't get back to where I had started. When I had made the cut I had had a good hold of the tonsil and had been holding it out from the side wall of the oropharynx. Now the tonsil had sprung back under the overlying muscle and I couldn't grasp it to pull it out again. Blood was filling the oropharynx. The nurse couldn't suck it out fast enough, and I couldn't see anything for red.

My pulse was rising. I had been feeling uncomfortable for a few minutes now, but only the familiar degree of uneasiness that is an almost daily part of surgical life. But suddenly, discomfort tipped into full-blown anxiety. My headlamp seemed painfully bright. I wanted to look away from its light, the very glare that was supposed to be illuminating things, and helping me. The scarlet sea in front of me, against the waxy foreground of my patient's chin, seemed to lose its colour. I could see its shininess but it might have been green because my retina seemed to have lost all connection to what lay in front. My perspective was also muddled so that I couldn't quite grasp the level of rising blood in comparison to the soft palate.

I had stopped putting swabs into my patient's mouth because they soaked through as soon as I introduced them, and only seemed to restrict the already small surgical field. I could see the criss-crossing weave in their fibre, designed for absorbency, highlighted by the ruby wetness of the blood. Like the blood was sporting itself on the weave, modelling texture with wetness.

A piece of flesh came away in my forceps and for a moment my heart lifted with the hope that what I had claimed was the tonsil itself. But when I snatched the suction from the nurse and held it deep into the soup and in a downwards, left direction, I saw I had just pulled a lump from the tonsil which still clamped itself to its home, like a mussel to a rock, bleeding in angry response to my attempts to remove it.

And then I lost my nerve. I saw the anaesthetist quietly asking her assistant for a bag of fluid, and I thought even the anaesthetist is alarmed, and I lost it. I turned for the first time ever since being left to operate unassisted, and I said to the scrub nurse and to everyone in the room, 'I can't manage. I need some help. Who is around?'

The mood in the room changed. It was out in the open. The theatre staff looked unnerved, and I imagined them thinking that things must be going badly because the surgeon was asking for help. Felisa, the nurse in charge of theatre that afternoon, stayed calm, though, and replied, 'I don't know which consultant is on call, but Miss Ngozi is in clinic,' and I felt relief enter my panicking heart like a draught. I saw her strict beautiful face oddly super-imposed on the spattering mess in front of me and I began to feel calm again. It was embarrassing to have to ask for help, but what more could I hope for than to have this sensible woman available? Someone I could successfully communicate my need to, just as she had recently taught me to on that course.

Already feeling brighter, I said, 'Please call her and tell

her I'm in trouble with a tonsillectomy and need her help.'
There would be no need for more than this. My message
was clear and I knew she would respond directly to it. I
saw Felisa leave theatre to make the call from the phone
just outside. My shame was out. My fear was out. I had
handed on the baton of responsibility, and my emotions
seemed suddenly my own again.

With a sense of having almost solved the problem by
just admitting to it, I elected to do no further damage, to
simply pack the patient's oropharynx. This would slow
her bleeding, and allow me to wait until Miss Ngozi
arrived to take over. Arranging tonsils swabs in both
fossae, I then filled the oropharynx until the swabs looked
like they were being spat out of her mouth. Like she had
bitten off more than she could chew from some big white
feast. And then I sat back.

I must have remained in this position, in a totally quiet
theatre, for three or four minutes. All of us waited for the
distinctive clippy step of Miss Ngozi in the corridor. For
the sight of her cap-framed face at the door. We did not
hear Felisa's soft padding to this door, so trained were all
our ears to the sound of a different step. And our eyes
were all expecting a tall woman to appear at the door, so
that when Felisa returned, we almost looked beyond her
for someone else. We might have ignored her altogether
had her voice and her message been less clear.

She cleared her throat and said, 'Miss Ngozi said thank
you for your message. But she is busy in clinic at the
moment and can't come.'

I was amazed. Querulously, I retorted, 'But I need her.
This is an emergency. Please call her again and explain
the situation to her properly.'

Firmly this time, Felisa replied, 'She is aware of the situation and will come at the end of clinic. She told me to tell you not to call anyone else.'

I opened my mouth under my steamy mask to try and enunciate in some other, more persuasive logic what seemed obvious to me. That this surgical emergency took precedence over the chronic niggles of the clinic. But Felisa had come right up to me now, and she concluded her speech at close range, out of the earshot of the others, 'She's not coming. She said to tell you JFDI.' Just fucking do it.

Surprise now eclipsed the sense of outrage I had just had, which in turn had replaced my previous panic. I knew everyone was looking at me and I knew that my eyelids' attempt to cup the tears forming there was being stretched. Everything was still. Everybody waited for my next move.

I took the Luc's forceps off the table next to me. They had dried blood on them. I began to pluck the swabs from my patient's mouth. The first ones, those on the outside, were polystyrene clean and squeaky. Then lower down, blood-dappled. And right at the end, puny little sops which dripped as I passed them over. Within a few flicks, I had taken out all but the swabs which actually lined the ravine of each tonsillar fossa. Going first for the right-hand side, I pulled out the last two bits of gauze which I had put there, and was relieved to find the area dry. The blood on these last two right-hand swabs must have come from the other side where I knew half a tonsil was still attached to the muscle bed.

With one thick grip, I pulled out the clump of swabs from the left-hand side. The half tonsil lay underneath them, an ugly thing, like a hunk of meat a dog has teethed a chunk out of. And blood still poured from its ragged surface, although I was grateful not to see any distinct arterial spurts.

The scrub nurse held the bipolar diathermy out for me, a schooled prompt for me to continue my careful dissection. My rejection by Miss Ngozi was still in my mind and I reached past my helpful colleague and grabbed the Gwynn-Evans, an instrument like a miniature rake but with piranha-sharp teeth. I used the forceps to pinch what I could of the messy tonsil remnant and applied the angry end of this tool to the patient's oropharynx. With a cross mind, a few scrapes and a good pull, I yanked the bleeding morsel out of my patient's mouth. I knew I was the worst kind of dilettante. I knew there had been no finesse or grace in my behaviour from the start of this case, but I also felt grateful for my anger which had made fear and anxiety impossible, which had pushed me on.

I was amazed to look down the beam of my spotlight on a happy scene. Within my patient's mouth, I could see the clean curve of the right tonsillar fossa now reflected on the left-hand side. No lumpy tonsil to see. And just one pretty stream of blood, coming from the tongue base on the left, like the ribbon from a trophy, decorating my long-awaited success. After such unruliness, it was a pleasure to apply the bipolar forceps to this furthest recess of the patient's mouth, clamp its arms together, press the pedal firmly with the ball of my foot and stem this stream with one short hiss.

I put the diathermy down and sat there, staring into the oropharynx, utterly in that world, standing there, looking as if at the familiar ghastly caves of some monstrous home. Nothing dripped or splashed or pumped or ran. It was over. Still feeling the hangover shame at my previous mistake and my melodramatic reaction to it, I let the gag down with a click of the metal clasp and saw the patient's jaws close in a bite. I checked the swab count tallied and felt the temporomandibular joints on both sides to make sure they had not been dislocated by the gag's protracted grip. I then unscrewed my headlight at the back and pulled it off the top of my head.

Everyone else was milling about in theatre, doing their thing. I tore my mask off, glad that no one was watching my face's unshielding. I found the patient's file and went to sit in the corner of theatre to write up my operation note. The anaesthetist was looking in the patient's mouth, about to extubate her, and I was glad to see that only a few drops of blood marked the inside of his clear plastic suction tube as he explored there.

I waited in theatre just long enough to see the tube come out and the patient wake up. Then, I limply thanked everyone and pulled the heavy door to exit this theatre and this horrible afternoon. The first thing I saw was Miss Ngozi sitting just outside at the vacant nurse's station, her briefcase open, a tidy block of letters in front of her, which she appeared to be reading and signing. She looked up brightly to my 'Miss Ngozi?' I pulled a chair out next to her and slumped into it. I felt ugly and uncontrolled next to her neatness, her collectedness.

'I knew you'd be fine,' she said, without prologue. 'And, next time, I think you'll know it too.' She put her notes in her little case and clicked it shut. I felt her palm on my arm very briefly and then was looking at her back disappearing down the corridor. Just before I lost sight of her at a corner, she turned and smiled. And in a raised whisper said, 'You're one of my girls!'

Poor communication, not clinical error, is the main reason why doctors end up getting sued. Because of this, we are increasingly taught, as surgeons, how better to relate to our patients. This is of course a good thing and we all need help here. By contrast, interacting with colleagues should be the easy bit, but occasionally is be-devilled by factors which are hard to pinpoint. Sex, power, competitiveness, enmity. And sometimes, even when we think we are communicating most clearly, we may be asking for the wrong thing. And the right answer to our question may be the one we least expect.

CHILDREN

Roughness is an absolute requirement of a surgeon. Not just because the specialty is competitive. Not only because we have to subdue humanity every time we stick the knife in. Even outside the operating theatre, surgeons often have to do unpleasant things to their patients in the name of greater clinical good.

Examples of this are manifold. In examining patients, we may have to cause pain to make a diagnosis. For example, there is an important clinical sign in abdominal examination called rebound, which involves applying steady manual pressure to an area of the patient's belly and then suddenly releasing one's hand. Causing the patient to wince is considered a positive finding, favouring a diagnosis of peritonitis.

In addition, plenty of the everyday procedures we perform in our work hurt. Draining an abscess is often done without an anaesthetic, since lignocaine is poorly effective in infected tissue and therefore hardly worth giving. Reducing fractures or dislocations of bones and joints in A&E is commonplace and often sore. And one of the most frequent jobs done by ENT doctors is nasal packing, in cases of severe nosebleed. This involves passing a urinary catheter into the nostril until it appears at the back of the mouth, and anchoring it there. And then using long, hard forceps to stuff the whole nasal cavity with gauze from the back to the front, a process which can cause significant suffering.

The ability to do these things demands a certain brutality, a characteristic for which surgeons have become historically renowned. Over the years, I have heard countless stories of men who revelled in making their juniors and patients cry, leaving nurses to deal with the emotional devastation they left in their wake. Thankfully, this breed is nearly extinct, and such behaviour has become not just outmoded, but downright unacceptable. There has been a cultural shift, and patients are demanding more from doctors than they used to. It is no longer enough to be technically proficient; nowadays, we need to be nice. And this presents the modern surgeon with a great challenge: how to combine a necessary degree of toughness with an equally important ability to be gentle.

Nowhere is this more necessary than in one's care of children. Instinctively, it might seem odd that roughness is ever called for in treating the underage patient. But, whether in examining or treating minors, we sometimes have to be unsentimental to get the job done. It is not comfortable for a child with appendicitis to have their abdomen palpated. Nor is it pleasant for a doctor to feel the neck of a child suffering with tonsillitis. But both are necessary to diagnosis and treatment.

Removing a foreign body from a toddler's nose provides another case in point. Inserting small objects into the nose is commonplace among little children. Often, by the time such a child reaches the hospital, a family member has had a go at removing the offending article, so that it has become lodged further back. As a surgeon, you can either attempt to remove the foreign body then and there with the child awake, or resort to giving them a general anaesthetic and do it in the operating theatre. For every reason in the book, the former is the preferable choice but requires a certain decisiveness.

The first time I was faced with this situation, I spent twenty minutes pointlessly attempting to persuade a four-year-old girl to lie still so that I could hook a barely visible bead out of her right nostril. Pleading was getting me nowhere. Observing my naivety, an experienced nurse came in and showed me what to do. After explaining her intention to the parents, she placed the girl's arms down at her sides and wrapped her up tightly in a hospital blanket, so that she looked like sausagemeat inside pastry. She lay the rigid roll of a screaming girl onto the bed, asked her father to hold her head still, and nodded to me to get the job done. With my charge so efficiently immobilised, it took me all of five seconds to flick the bead free from her nose with my Jobson Horn Probe, and a much relieved family left the department a few minutes later.

Unfortunately, the occasional need to be rough with a sick or injured minor in order to help them is not confined to this sort of case. There are times when I have had to muster all my courage to do something horrible to a child in the name of good doctoring. I remember one of these times in particular.

During my six months in A&E, each doctor spent a month working in the paediatric emergency room which abutted the adult department. This specialist unit took infants and children from a large area of the city. As juniors, our brief was clear. Anyone under the age of one should be seen directly by a paediatrician. Anyone else could be assessed by a novice, one of us.

I was sitting behind the paediatric admissions desk one afternoon, heart full of dread, looking at the hapless babies all around me waiting to be seen. Hoping against hope that they were all less than twelve months old, that they were too young and fragile to be seen by a doctor as unschooled as me. When the trauma phone rang.

I answered it. The call came from a paramedic in an ambulance that was traffic-slicing its way to our unit. He told me we should prepare for the arrival of Elena who was ten years old and had broken her leg. They would be with us in two minutes. I conveyed the message to the nurse in charge. A room was cleared in readiness and a call put out to the duty orthopaedic surgeon. The parents waiting to be seen with their babies looked discomfited, witnessing our alertness, realising perhaps that this is what medical staff look like when they are expecting the arrival of a child who really is ill. And they seemed to hold their babies closer, as if wanting to keep them from whatever was about to happen.

Then she was there, the child I had been told about. There was the strange dissonance of this sort of arrival.

The real paramedics replacing the imagined ones. The smell and look of constructively harried humans. The snaking of cold air, brought in from the outside, working its way into the over-warm corners of the children's A&E. The hyperacoustic noise of new voices, clanking metal, and the squeaking of rubber wheels and shoe soles. Foremost in this din were the cries of a child who was not just making a fuss.

One of the paramedics told the story. Elena had been playing with her sister in their garden. They had a climbing frame with swings and a trapeze. They had been taking turns to twist the trapeze and then hang from it as it unravelled. During Elena's go, and in the shrieking dizzy joy of an unwinding, she had put one foot down. Instead of scuffing the dirt and spinning on with the rest of her, this foot had become caught in a divot in the ground, immobilising her leg while her body had continued with the momentum of its twirling. Elena's mother had called an ambulance immediately on seeing how badly her daughter was hurt. The paramedic added that they were running fluid and morphine through the child's intravenous drip. The child's mother was parking and would be in directly.

The paramedics left and I found myself alone with Elena. After all the flurry, the sudden stillness of the room dumbfounded me and I wasn't sure what to do. Blood had already been sent off, the analgesia had been taken care of. In my search for useful inspiration, only the most irrelevant thoughts beset me. Among them was the narcissistic observation that this girl reminded me of myself at her age. Her frame, her hair, the humourless intensity of her brow. And I also noticed her deep pain, which came in starts. A silent score, interspersed with sudden short plaintive cries. As if this child's clean brain was learning a new circuit, and was having to acknowledge repeatedly that the world could be this awful. She was holding a stuffed rabbit, like a black version of the velveteen rabbit from that sad story. At some stage later, Elena told me this toy was called Snowy.

I didn't think there was any point embarking on taking a history until Elena's mother arrived. My patient was clearly in too much pain to give me one. But the idea of examining her paralysed me. How could I possibly touch this child's leg when she was already in agony, when to do so would make her feel worse? As if in answer to my thoughts, I heard the calm voice of Mr Renlow, one of the young orthopaedic surgeons, behind me saying, 'No need to touch her. Just look. She's fractured her femur.'

I felt a great relief at the arrival of this man, whom I had met several times over a trauma patient. He was more experienced than me, and I felt happily usurped. But my relief was short-lived.

My handsome colleague had invited me to look at our patient's injury, and in so doing, I had noticed what I had not seen before. Elena's shorts-clad legs were asymmetrical. The left one had the pretty contour the eye expected, although it shook in sympathy with its partner. The afflicted right leg also looked straight from ankle to knee. But, above this level, the thigh looked strange and widened, as if it was not following one line. The femur, that beautiful longest of bones in the body, seemed derailed. And in the middle of the thigh was an area where there seemed to be an extra joint, a corner pressing against the soft tissue where there should have been only straightness.

'We need to reduce the fracture. Stop the soft tissue damage getting any worse,' said Mr Renlow. 'Then we can sort out some X-rays and go from there. Looks like a classic spiral fracture. You hold the top of the leg, I'll get it back in position.'

On hearing his words, Elena began to scream, stopping only for breaths. A nurse came in and went over to the other side of the bed from where we were. She took the girl's hand and murmured reassuringly to her.

I wanted to go over to the nurse's side. I wanted to hold the young girl's hand and stroke it, and comfort her. I wanted to be on the good guys' team. But my head was telling me to do my job, to assist the orthopaedic registrar in whatever he deemed surgically necessary. As I reached out my hands to the child's leg, she turned to me and said, 'Don't touch me. Please don't touch me,' just as I made contact with her. One of my hands held her hip. With the other, I viced the top of her thigh and there seemed to be a brief hiatus before there came the sickening sound of Elena shouting, and the sickening feeling of grating under my hand, as my colleague pushed the two divorced pieces of bone back into rightful unity.

The process took seconds, and before I had time to look around me, to look inside myself, Mr Renlow had clicked the brakes off the bed, and was nodding to me to help him wheel the bed out of the room and towards the X-ray department. Later that afternoon, he showed me the films, demonstrating a perfect spiral femoral fracture, a black line corkscrewing its way down the length of the white bone. He told me that she would go for pinning and plating of her leg that day, and that his consultant was optimistic she would get a good result. Because we had realigned her thigh, soft tissue damage had been minimal.

Compared to this, the need for gentleness when dealing with children would seem philosophically obvious. Indeed, considering a child's well-being has become paramount in medical and surgical care. Paediatric units are no longer the sparse, unfriendly places they used to be. Parents aren't chased from the wards any more when their children have to stay overnight. Hospital staff are encouraged to discard white coats, formal titles and any other vestiges of their position that might intimidate youngsters. In many hospitals, children on their way to have an operation are allowed to drive motorised toy cars to theatre, to make that transit more enjoyable, to distract them from their journey's end.

But, obvious and necessary as it is, knowing when and how to be gentle with children is not always easy. If adult patients are sometimes ill-equipped to ask for the kindness they need, children can be even more baffling in this regard. Babies at least cry, and in so doing, let you know there's something you're not getting right. Such signs may be very hard to interpret in older children.

I remember clearly the case of a child to whom I failed to show the compassion I should have. He was a boy called Ben and, like Elena, he was ten years old. He had been admitted to the hospital with severe headaches on a day when I was on call. My registrar had left his stethoscope by the boy's bed by mistake, and as a pretext for asking me to go and get it for him, he suggested I check that Ben was comfortable before the night set in. I felt rueful about the request. Never mind that my senior was treating me like his slave, I never did enjoy going to see kids. I didn't know how to talk to them, and felt that they didn't like me.

I made my way reluctantly up to the children's ward. A nurse guarded its entrance and, once in, I asked her where I would find Ben. On the way to his bed, I passed a colourful mural amongst whose characters I recognised a fish called Nemo. And I passed an auxiliary serving out the evening meal from a jolly trolley which had been shaped and painted to look like Thomas the Tank Engine.

The six-bedded room that Ben was in was called Green Bay, and accordingly it had been decorated like a jungle. The walls were papered with exotic trees and brightly populated by all manner of lurid animals and birds. Within this cheerful environment, Ben immediately stood out. He wasn't watching one of the televisions which stretched down in front of each bed on a corrugated neck. And unlike the other children, Ben had no parent with him. He sat alone and cross-legged on top of his covers, wearing paisley pyjamas. This old-man pattern was in swirling purples, and a maroon collar and ankle trim helped the eye know the theme in among all the whirling confusion. His back was the child's effortless perpendicular. His feet were bare. He had a book on his lap, and was reading. My registrar's stethoscope lay next to him on his bed.

I approached him awkwardly. Seeing me, he closed his book and I saw that it was by Susan Cooper, and suppressed the urge to ask him if I could have a look, I had so enjoyed her stories as a child. Instead, I introduced myself by my Christian name, as one is meant to with children. He didn't tell me his name in turn, but just looked straight back at me, waiting to see what I would say to him next, which was to ask him where his parents were. Ben told me his mother had gone home. He explained that he had three younger brothers whom she had to look after, and that his dad was away on business.

Seeing an already comprehensive history and examination written by the registrar in the notes, I told Ben I had just been asked to pop up and check he was comfortable before the night began. He nodded, and with a great sense of relief, I picked up my registrar's stethoscope and left the ward, a mere five minutes after entering it.

On-call nights vary between the extremes of quiet and hectic, but the worst are those that fall in between. Sleeping all night because there are no jobs to do feels like grace on the rare occasions that it happens. Being so busy that you don't go near your on-call bed has a kind of momentum that is OK too. But this night was neither fish nor fowl. Summonses came singly to sort things out on wards or in A&E. I had no list of things to do, and every completed job tempted an ensuing rest. But, so far, my bleep had kept up a steady monologue of querulous calls, each perfectly timed with the end of one task to give news of the next.

I finally pressed the open-sesame combination of numbers on my on-call room door just before three in the morning. I cleaned my teeth and took off my shoes. I cleared the pile of bloke's magazines from the top of the bedside cabinet and chucked them in the doorless cupboard, on top of the mucky scrubs and old shoes and wire coat hangers that gathered dust there. And then, standing by the bed, I winkled both hands up the back of my scrub top and unhooked my bra, to let me sleep more comfortably without taking off what I would only have to put back on again when summoned from my bed.

I climbed under the thin blanket and onto the sheet-covered foam mattress, thinking of boarding-school beds. And, irrelevantly, a Thomas Hardy line crossed my mind, though I could not think where it belonged. 'Make my lone bed hard – Would 'twere underground!'

Once lying down, I unclipped my bleep and put it on the bedside unit with my pen and a piece of paper, knowing how necessary it is for me to write down what I am told over the phone if a call wakes me from sleep. How hard it is to go from slumber to instant clinical response. And then I switched off the light. I didn't turn over. I knew I would need a few moments lying on my back to unwind before attempting sleep. Almost instantly, the hypnagogic softness of the room sharpened again to yet another bleep.

I looked at the fluorescent face of my watch, which told me I had only been resting for two minutes. I switched on the light, in whose bulb I imagined the coiled filaments had probably not yet completely darkened with desuetude, and checked the short grey screen of my bleep to see what number I needed to call. I was hoping it might be some telephone advice that was required. Or at worst, a visit to A&E, a mere stone's throw from where I lay.

The extension number I called reached its destination. The phone there was answered by a nurse who was on the children's ward, in the furthest recess of the hospital from the now deliciously comfortable cot in which I lay. She told me they needed me to come up and see Ben, whose pain relief wasn't working and who couldn't sleep. I said I'd be straight up and put the phone down. Then I lay back once more in the bed, momentarily, just long enough to imprint on my every fibre the deeply comfortable repose I was about to drag myself from.

I sat up, refastened my bra, and slid on my shoes. I picked up my bleep, pen and paper and trudged out of my room. On my way out to the main hospital corridor, I passed through the doctors' mess where, within the signature polystyrene landscape of fast-food detritus, several bodies lay awkwardly on chairs, fast asleep, and a young female doctor with pretty make-up ate curry from a foil box. A few minutes later, I arrived outside the children's ward, a dimmed version of where I had been earlier that evening. Through the glass gaps of the decorated door, I could see Nemo's bossed head and the Thomas the Tank Engine trolley, parked up against one of the walls, still grinning darkly.

I presented myself through the intercom system and, hearing its buzzed salute, passed through the door and stopped at the reception desk just inside the ward. A night nurse sat under a desk light, eating a doughnut and leafing through a celebrity magazine, whose pages crackled with sugar as she turned them.

'I've come to see Ben,' I said.

She looked up, not at me, but at the whiteboard on the wall behind me, which had all the kids' names on it and then, just faintly turning her head and eyes towards the nurses' coffee room behind her, called out, 'Green Bay. Bed six?'

About ten seconds later, a young nurse appeared. Her cartoon name badge read Julie. She looked awake and efficient, and we smiled at one another. Within this greeting, there passed a mutual acknowledgement that we were not enemies. That we were both professional women.

That she was not going to make things hard for me just because she happened to be a nurse, and I a doctor. Then she said, 'He's been fine most of the night. We haven't really heard from him. He's a pretty quiet kind of boy. Then, about an hour ago he started crying. Says his head's really hurting. That he can't sleep. Observations and neuro obs are all stable. I just think he's sore.'

She added that Ben had been written up for oral morphine, but that this prescription was not on the part of the drug chart that allowed them to give it regularly, and that the dose was small. She passed me a children's drug formulary and looked companionably over my shoulder as I searched for oromorph in its index. I flicked to the right page and saw that Ben had only been written up for about half of what he was entitled to. My heart lifted with the prospect that this would be a quick and straightforward visit, that I would be back in bed soon.

Julie said that Ben's drug chart was at the end of his bed, so I made my way down the short corridor to Green Bay, where I had been earlier that evening. The jungle mural on its walls looked less cheerful now, reminding me of the slightly menacing forest that becomes the world all around in *Where the Wild Things Are*. I almost had to feel my way among the six beds because it was dark and most of the curtains had been drawn, making my path uncertain in front of me. The three beds on the left were obscured by these curtains, the only noise coming from them a single snore, the soft snuffling of a sweet young pharynx.

On the right, the first two beds were only partly screened from view, their curtains still slightly open. In the first, I saw a father sharing the narrow bed with his toddler daughter. She had a cast on her arm which poked out from their hug, and they both appeared to be deeply asleep. In the next cubicle, a boy slept alone in a bed while his mother lay next to him, across three plastic chairs that she must have dragged in from the corridor. A coat was folded under her head and her right arm lay across her child's mattress against his sleeping body.

Beyond this last curtain, which seemed solid as a wall in the darkness, lay Ben. His bedside light was on. He lay on his side facing the window, back to me. His legs were pulled up to his stomach and through the dated paisley chaos of his pyjama top, I could make out the more even pattern of his vertebral bones, running down the middle of his thin back. He held a bunched-up combination of sheet and blanket close to his chest, where a soft toy might have been. The plastic chair which belonged to his cubicle stood between him and the window and one of his arms was stretched across its hard orange surface.

He must have heard me coming, for just as I noticed this arm, he flexed it back into his body. I passed around the bottom of his bed, taking the cardboard drugs chart from its slot there as I did so, and then I sat down on the chair, which felt chilly through the cotton of my scrubs. Some distant part of my memory registered an association between being about the age of the boy in front of me, and feeling this same coldness on my bottom from the surface of an institutional chair.

Unlike earlier, Ben looked up at me and said a quiet hello. He looked younger to me in the night.

'The nurse tells me your head hurts,' I said in a voice that I tried to pitch somewhere between a voice for a baby and a voice for an adult, and so sounded inauthentic.

He nodded, looking briefly at me and then beyond me to the featureless window. His chin had wrinkled a bit, and seemed to promise tears, and I understood this, the way that someone else putting your pain in words can make you want to cry. I also knew that I would prefer it if he didn't, because I was still thinking hopefully of the warm bed I had just left.

'Is the pain the same as before but worse, or is it a different feeling?' I asked, and he said, 'The same.'

'Well, I'm going to increase the amount of painkiller you can have,' I said. 'And then you can get some sleep. In the morning, we'll get to the bottom of what's making you feel so unwell.'

This boy, who had seemed so soft to me a moment before, appeared withdrawn again, offering me no response. He was still and silent. I felt at a loss, and exhausted, and even a little afraid although I could not think why. I looked at my watch. It was 3.30 in the morning. I didn't want to fumble about any longer. The knowledge that this boy was having a bad time was something I felt more in my head than my heart. I longed for the snug dereliction of my on-call room.

So I changed Ben's drug chart, increasing his oromorph dose, writing on the part of the chart which showed it was to be given regularly. I patted Ben's shoulder, the brusque pat I had learned from countless surgical seniors, and was surprised by how small his bones felt under my palm. I made my way from his bed, out of the bay and back down the corridor, to the ward's exit.

Julie was there, and thanked me warmly for having come down so promptly. The gentle sincerity of her thanks, so unusual in a day's work, replaced the uneasy feeling I had in my heart, with a pleasing sense of being a hard-working doctor, up at all hours. I went back to my on-call room and slept deeply until the real morning arrived soon afterwards.

When I got up, and just before going home to get some proper sleep, I sat down with the registrar who was about to do the first ward round of the day, and I told her about the events of the night, among them my visit to Ben. I told her that I had upped his morphine, and also found myself saying that there had been something else about this boy that had made me uncomfortable. That he had given me a bad feeling. I did not say that I suspected this was guilt at having given so little to a child, whose needs I couldn't fathom, but whom I knew was suffering.

I learned later that week that Ben had died. He had not even made it as far as having a scan done. A post-mortem had shown a rare brain tumour, a pineoblastoma. The associated hydrocephalus from this tumour had killed Ben quite suddenly. During his short stay in hospital, he had not complained much and consequently no one had taken his symptoms all that seriously.

I still feel ashamed of how I behaved that night. Certainly I was tired. Perversely, I may have argued to myself that ten years was plenty old enough to be spending the night alone since at this same age I was spending all of my nights unparented. I may even have sensed that death was in the room, as I have done a few times since becoming a doctor. And may, as a consequence, have had an atavistic desire to get away from this child, already in death's embrace.

But, since having my own children, I have come to a closer understanding of the source of my unease. I know

now that when a sick child cries in the night, medicine is the last thing on their mind. And that what Ben needed from me that night was to give him whatever small amount of my heart's warmth I could afford. Without a parent nearby, and in the appalling solipsism of his pain, Ben sought the nearness of another person, a need to which he was too young to give a voice. And he was unable to find this comfort in me.

One of the things that people often ask surgeons is how we can bear to cut people open, how we can be so ruthless. Certainly, a lack of sentimentality, an ability to quell emotional doubt and act decisively is a cardinal surgical quality, without which one simply cannot do the job. And this may require one to steel oneself occasionally, despite a more natural instinct to be soft.

But a good surgeon also needs to know how to be gentle. How to subdue the toughness which becomes such an indelible part of our professional persona. If we do not, we will fail our patients, who may look to us in the most terrifying moments of their lives as the only available source of human comfort. At no time is this more crucial than in one's surgical management of the very young.

APPEARANCES

Whichever surgical specialty you choose, there are small as well as big operations to be learned. General surgeons have to cure piles as well as colon cancer. Orthopaedic surgeons need to fix ingrowing toenails, as well as save limbs. The neurosurgeon has to sort out as many back-aches as brain tumours.

When I started training in ear, nose and throat surgery, I thought that learning cosmetic procedures was the price that had to be paid for an altogether more valuable apprenticeship in head and neck cancer surgery. Like most youngsters, I aspired to be a big, life-saving surgeon, not someone who made people look pretty. So I was disappointed when I was asked one Saturday to go and assist in an operation that sat uneasily with my simplistic outlook. A facelift.

Not having yet assisted in any of this kind of surgery had not stopped me feeling quite sanctimonious about it.

I had an unformulated aversion to private-sector hospitals, where most of these operations are performed, and an equally raw sense that reconstructing a woman's face in order to make her look better was part of some patriarchal conspiracy that I was duty-bound to protest against.

In addition, I had heard a mixed press about the surgeon I was due to help. Rufus Wells had trained in the US and had brought the expertise he had garnered there home to his native Britain. He was known as an old-school practitioner with a vast operative repertoire, and as a womaniser. He wasn't popular, partly owing to his huge local private practice, but was acknowledged by all to be an excellent surgeon.

As I set off in my car that Saturday, I was thinking how I was wasting my time. I had no interest in learning an operation which I felt was immoral, and in any case thought I was unlikely to get any real cutting experience, since the patient would want the consultant she was paying richly for to do everything. An hour later, I pulled into the appointed private hospital's driveway. I noticed the prosperous car-on-gravel sound this made, and felt cross that I should have anything to do with such a noise. I felt both responsible and not responsible for it, like when your stomach rumbles when you least want it to and you feel somehow let down by yourself.

On entering the hospital, I was pleasantly surprised by the novelty of being greeted by the receptionist, who said I could park free right outside, and asked after my journey as if I had crossed the world to do my duty. I felt gratified but suppressed these feelings, as I went upstairs to the room where I had been told I would find Mr Wells and our facelift patient.

I paused briefly outside this chamber before leaning forwards to open its door. The weight of the sententious thoughts I had been thinking must have made me open it with extra gusto, because I made a little burst onto the scene. I caused just enough ruckus that both of the room's inhabitants must have responded to the sudden shift of air caused by the heavy door being thrown open, and turned towards it. Because they were both facing me as I came in, I was able to see very clearly the familiar figure of Mr Wells and the unfamiliar one. Who seemed doubly new to me in that first moment because this patient was not the overly made-up, vain-looking middle-aged woman I had expected, but instead a compact and completely bald little man.

I had no need to collect myself, to stutter out any introduction. The urbane Mr Wells, addressing his charge by his Christian name with winning familiarity, said, 'Louis, this is my surgical assistant for the day.' The way he referred to and looked at me didn't give me any of the sense of pride I usually have when reminded of the professional club I have been able to join, but instead made me feel very female and small, although there was something not altogether unpleasant about this diminishing. I felt like some tasty, wholly inadequate thing, some dated maid. It is peculiar how some men can both reduce and lift you, in a way you don't resent, despite your brain telling you that you should.

Perhaps the patient sensed some awkwardness in me, for he cut straight back to where he must have been in the conversation with Mr Wells that I had interrupted, in a way which included me. He jumped straight over any preamble. So we missed out on having to get me from an awkward social place to a comfortable one by just leaping straight into that comfortable zone. This struck me as accomplished, and as a kindness.

What he said, looking at my consultant, was, 'Your boss has been trying to persuade me that I shouldn't be having this surgery, because I've got no hair to hide the scars in.' His voice was the same soft East Coast one Mr Wells had. They must have met over there. 'I've been telling him, this country's rubbing off on him if he's started to turn patients away. Any anyways, he hasn't won me over. I'm sticking to my guns and Rufus is the one I want.'

He said all of this with his eyes on Mr Wells, but his face was tilted somewhere between my consultant and me. And this gave me a small chance to look at his face, that part of him that he was happy for someone to make bleed, that he wanted cut and corrected. It was a short opportunity, although long enough because his syllables were spoken slowly in a lovely way that seemed only semi-foreign to me, and honeyed not just by money, but by confident maleness.

His sixty-year-old face was like this. It was quite round and small. And the skin did seem loose around its small-ness, although I probably only noticed this because I was thinking of facelifts. It was as if a well-appointed drawing room had been hung with too-heavy curtains. This gave our patient a slight jowliness. And there were bags under the eyes, and wrinkles above them. Nonetheless, this man's ageing face suited him, and had that pleasing segmented appearance that ageing male faces do if they have not been ruined by booze. The skin seems to keep its firm-ness, but to become separated into parcels, whereas with women the whole thing just collapses.

So here were these segments in this small but hand-some face. The crescentic eye bags, which he wanted taken away, the cheek divided by a deep but handsome nasolabial groove. Here was a pretty cubist painting. And the segments fitted with the texture of his skin, a weathered but polished look, leading from face to neck. At the suprasternal notch, just before the sky-blue cambric hospital gown stopped the view, there was that speckled texture of man's neck skin, reddish brown with white pinpoint prickles in it.

The body this face belonged to was also small, and the two big parts matched each other. Sitting up in bed, erect, the patient was still shorter than my consultant, even though Mr Wells was positioned semi-slouched over his patient's notes. There was a window behind them, and behind this a tree with so many tiny leaves being blown on it that the foliage was like a crowd of people laughing their heads off, but the branches were thick and motionless. The two men's heads were in a completely different relationship to this wooden, arbitrary measuring line that appeared to my eye. One beneath, one above.

But all of these accidental physical observations seemed less noticeable to me than the likeability of the patient. While I had been musing, Mr Wells had started to draw some lines with a purple pen, around where the man's hairline might have been, to show the patient where the scar would sit, the scar which would usually be hidden in hair which was not there, which he didn't have.

And our patient was doing something in response to the touch of this felty purple nib. The pen touching his face. This contact had begun something for him. As if the process of whatever change he had dreamed of had begun. He had tilted his head back at a just-Adam's-apple-whitening angle. Just that much. And had closed his eyes as if in anticipation of the longer sleep to come, or in a dream-like way, dreaming of some new self. His face was offered up. His lips were pursed, which eased out the deep grooves and made me think of a drag queen, or a pierrot, or a woman's face held forward for nightly cold cream. Or indeed of any face that is gesturing towards being another kind of face, a face that it is not.

The psychological openness of revealing himself like this softened me utterly towards this man. His eyes-shut time was short, and the purple lines were drawn and done, and his eyes were open again. Mr Wells was nodding OK to his patient, who was saying he didn't care about the scars.

'Just shape it up for me, Rufus,' he said. 'And, I hope you'll let your protégée do some of the handiwork.'

'Well, that is an offer,' said Mr Wells, smiling. And he put the signed consent form in the notes, and the notes on the table at the end of the bed, perfectly squarely, all the corners of cardboard in line with all the corners of wood. We said a triangular sort of goodbye, and Mr Wells pushed the heavy door open for me and held it so that I had to pass under his arm, oranges-and-lemons style. Then we walked together down the corridor to the changing rooms.

'Do you know why he wants it done?' I asked, because I had rehearsed this question on my drive in, so felt I should ask it. Mr Wells replied, 'I don't get too worked up about motivations. I tell them, this isn't gonna change your life. I make sure they don't seem completely insane. That's it. Beyond that, if they want it done, I'll do it.'

As I heard this answer, I realised I cared less about what my consultant said than I had earlier that morning, when I had thought about interrogating him on the moral aspects of cosmetic surgery on my drive in from home. The fact was that simply liking the patient had made me less interested in the whys and wherefores of what he was having done. Would I have sat higher on my high horse if I had found this man less sympathetic? Was that all that my sensibilities boiled down to?

There was no need for a combination lock to get through the door of the women's changing room, reminding me of E. M. Forster's saying that 'Trust is a luxury in which only the wealthy can indulge.' Anything left unlocked in an NHS changing room would be stolen within minutes. I stepped into the cool cream space in which I was to get ready. Despite myself, I felt a flush of pleasure at the prettiness of the room, which would have embarrassed me had I not been completely alone. The room was painted dusty pink. There were neat piles of scrubs on pine shelves and these uniforms were also pink instead of the blue I had always had before. And there were shiny lockers for permanent staff, and another bank of lockers for visitors, which had sparkly keys hanging from their locks with the hospital's name, and 'Welcome'.

To add to the sense of luxury, there were three different styles of surgical cap from which to choose, named 'Flair', 'Chic' and 'Miss'. I chose one from the pile because it was the same as the NHS ones I had been wearing for years. And around a corner were clean loos and basins. And the mirrors above these were circled with lights, like those in actresses' dressing rooms. And each basin had a basket full of soap and hand cream next to it. In truth, I could have spent all day there.

I selected and put on some scrubs which felt unusual because the trousers had a tailored feel to them and were gathered in at the ankle. I didn't just look different, a softened version of the surgeon I was, I felt different in my skin too. This costume brought out something unfamiliar in me, like high heels and a dress do to even the least feminine of girls.

I followed the directions I had been given to theatre, and Mr Wells was the first thing I noticed as I went in. He was sitting in a chair right in front of the door, framed to my view. He was sitting as only men can do, with his legs wide apart, briefcase resting on great square knees, tan showing at his ankles. And behind him was a glass window, looking out onto the hospital gardens below, the only window I have ever seen in an operating theatre.

The scrubs he wore were midnight blue, and very dark in that sunlit room. I felt very pink indeed when I saw this deep blueness. I felt like a woman in a sanitary towel advert. I thought he and I could stand on top of a surgically themed wedding cake, we looked so very male and so very female.

We scrubbed silently together and approached the table, where our patient awaited, lying like a perfect blue effigy. The anaesthetist was fussing over him, tucking this wire in here, adjusting the height of the table. Checking the position of the tube. Like a parent preening an already tidy child on their way to school for the first time.

Mr Wells began by injecting the patient's face all over with combination of lignocaine and adrenaline, to keep bleeding to a minimum. You could see that he was in precisely the right plane with this local anaesthetic. You could see the hydrostatic pressure of the liquid lifting the skin off its underlying musculature. And he then draped our patient, with a lifting and swirling of the drapes, with such a sinuous winding, and such a perfect snug clipping, that I was reminded of what I had noticed a few times before, that you can tell a gifted surgeon by the grace which accompanies even the most pedestrian of the tasks that surround their operating.

Mr Wells began with the eyelid surgery, concentrating on the upper lids first. Having marked out a tiny fold in each upper lid with a pen, he used a fine pair of forceps to hold this delicate bagginess away from the eye, and then cut this away with a fine diathermy needle. I watched as each tiny crescent of skin came away from the eyelid, held away from the eye with forceps as it was taken off. This bit of skin on each side was so very small and light that it fell in on itself, stuck to itself, like cobwebs do when you brush them with a hand. Congealingly. And no blood was left behind. Just the whitish crescent of a deskinned eyelid, like a tiny icy pond you might skate on with miniature skates.

Once these little bits of skin were removed, Mr Wells asked for a 6.0 suture, as fine as a blonde hair, and sewed up both little gapes, each one of which looked like a separate wall eye. A similar procedure was performed on the lower lids, although here the orbicularis oculi muscle around the eye was also hitched up to the orbital periosteum to give extra tightness. What remained at the end of all the eye cuts were four hardly perceptible lines, which Mr Wells said would fade and become invisible within a couple of weeks.

Over the next few hours, Mr Wells performed a most beautiful facelift. I say this, not because I have seen many others, but because I have never seen better surgery anywhere. At every stage of the operation, my consultant explained what he was doing, showed me the hazards that accompanied each specific step. And, remembering his patient's wishes, he handed me my own fine suture when all the important work had been done, so that I too could sew up some of the newly tightened face.

After the operation was done, and while Mr Wells stopped

to thank the theatre staff and talk to the anaesthetist, I crossed the room to find our patient's notes and write him up for some post-operative analgesia. The drug chart was in the middle of the file, and I opened it on a page covered in neat writing recording the surgeon's discussion with the patient about the pros and cons of facelift surgery.

As I sat there, writing up the medication, I looked back on the way I had felt that morning, recalling the un-informed judgements I had made about the probity of cosmetic surgery. And I felt foolish in remembering my earlier feelings. What I now saw was that the surgery I had assisted in that day had been surgery at its moral best. Surgery where there had been a full and transparent understanding between doctor and patient. Surgery conducted in comfort, with all the right equipment, and with no time pressure. Surgery done beautifully.

I have rarely seen higher surgical standards than I did that day. And, by the same token, the more dubious things I have witnessed as a surgeon have not been confined to a particular kind of procedure, or hospital. Even in the ostensibly superior environment of life-saving operations, I have seen consultants take credit for operations their juniors have performed. I have seen incomplete cancer excisions passed off as complete successes. And every other kind of dishonesty there is.

All of this has led me to the conclusion that there is no such thing as a moral or an immoral operation. That the sanctity of surgery comes from an honest communi-cation between a doctor and their patient who, in the operating theatre at least, is completely at their mercy. And that surgical virtue or lack of it comes from who is holding the knife, not where it is put.

CHANGES

The further you get as a doctor, the narrower your area of clinical expertise becomes. The joke goes that you start out as a house officer who knows nothing about everything, and end up being a consultant who knows everything about nothing. From a patient's point of view, the advantage of seeing a specialist is obvious: once you know what disease or injury you have, you want to be treated by the person who knows the most about it.

But, there are shortcomings in the system of specialisation too. As with any form of taxonomy, there are some things which are not easily classified. A patient with nebulous symptoms may take a long time to be referred to the right specialist. And, as doctors, a preoccupation with our own specialty may lead us to overlook the wider clinical picture. We may discover that the problem we are attending to is not the thing that needs fixing at all.

Dizziness is a good example of a symptom which confounds easy classification. No one area of medicine can lay claim to this symptom, nor is there a single school of clinicians to whom GPs can reliably refer patients who have it. Although ENT surgeons receive the majority of these cases, they also fall under the care of neurologists, cardiologists, and psychiatrists, to name but a few.

Woe betide the dizzy patient who is referred to the wrong specialist. If I see someone with this presenting complaint, the first thing I want to establish is whether they have been correctly referred to ENT. I do not have the time or the expertise to treat anyone whose dizziness is not of otolaryngological origin. With this in mind, I begin by asking a patient if their giddiness is rotatory in nature, whether it feels a bit like being on roundabout. Or if it is more like the faint feeling you have if you stand up too fast in a hot bath. If the patient has true rotatory vertigo, I proceed. If not, I wrap things up as quickly as I can, and refer the person back to their general practitioner, who may then send them on to a different kind of clinician.

Usually, this system works and most people end up in the correct doctor's room. If you have a sharp GP, you may even be lucky enough to see the right person first off. But the situation is far from ideal. Dizzy patients who have been sent to me in error are understandably peeved when they discover I have lost interest in them just because their complaint doesn't happen to lie within my precise clinical remit. Some have waited weeks to see me, and they may have to wait again before seeing someone else.

Occasionally, though, our narrow adherence to the organ system in which we have been expertly schooled proves to be not just inconvenient but life-threatening. The recent experience of a family friend who also happens to be a doctor illustrates this as well as any story I know.

Tony recently attended his local A&E suffering from severe abdominal pain. He was admitted under the general surgeons, the specialists responsible for problems occurring in this part of the body. Despite being seen by the most senior general surgery consultant available, and having the full battery of tests, a diagnosis could not be reached. Two days later, and with no improvement in my friend's condition, a decision was made to perform an exploratory laparotomy, an operation which involves cutting open the abdomen from chest to groin and examining all the organs inside. Still none of the experts could find anything wrong with him. There was no appendicitis and no problem with the gut or liver. The spleen and pancreas looked healthy.

Within four days of his admission, Tony was struggling for his life in the intensive care unit. By this stage, his whole body was packing up, and a lung scan was organised to investigate his respiratory function, which had started to deteriorate. Huge blood clots in both of his lungs were revealed. These potentially fatal pulmonary emboli were clearly the cause of his original abdominal pain. Anticoagulant treatment was started at this late stage, and luckily he survived.

This is a clear example of how the organisation of doctors into clinical specialties can be hazardous as well as beneficial. The best general surgeons couldn't find what the most ordinary of respiratory physicians might have discovered much sooner.

But it is not only strictly physical problems which present

themselves to doctors under other guises. I met Aidan one summer during a clinic entirely devoted to people with nose problems, the rhinology clinic. The morning had started well. The first two patients I saw had simple problems. One of them was suffering from rhinitis and needed some steroid nasal spray. Another, with a long history of nasal polyps, had come to discuss the possibility of sinus surgery. Both were pleasant company, and told clear stories of the difficulties they were having with their nose. Neither of them had any comorbidities, nothing to confound or complicate their specific rhinological disorders. I felt a lightness of exchange with these patients, a happiness which came from the satisfaction of treating straightforward problems properly.

I thought the third set of notes I was given by the nurse must belong to a child, because it was so slim. Its cover still had the sheen that cardboard has before it goes soft and hairy, and as I put the folder down on my desk it pinged open with newness to reveal a white A4 card from the medical photography department, entitled 'Rhinoplasty views'. Underneath these words were three photos of a young man. One taken from each side, criminal style, and one from the front with the camera pointing up the nose from underneath, to illustrate the nasal tip.

My patient's hair was brown and thick, and was not just cut but styled. It was layered and the sections were short and spiky at the top, feathering forward over the brow, lying in front of the ears like sideburns. His collar seemed to have been turned up for the photo, and I noticed it was fine and silky, like the collar of a blouse.

I reminded myself that this was a rhinology session, that the focus of these pictures was meant to be the patient's nose. So, I directed my eyes to that organ, to discover what might be abhorrent about it. Huge? Deformed by a fight? No. The nose I saw was regular, even pretty for a man. In fact, the angle of its projection was sufficiently turned up that one might have mistaken it for a girl's nose had it not sat in this particular face. It had a small hump and the tip was symmetrical and pleasing. I couldn't see why someone would want to change it.

The nurse asked Aidan in. He came in softly but not apologetically. He didn't display any of the self-consciousness patients often do. A self-consciousness about walking into a domain that is so much someone else's, but in which you must yourself occupy centre stage. An apprehensiveness any one of us might feel going in to see a doctor, to behold their intimately foreign face, to smell the smell of their last patient, to understand in this smelling of someone else, one's own repeatability, one's own lack of importance. Nor did he do the opposite. He did not turn shyness into reflex bravado as some do, puffing out a pigeon-chest, plumping down in a chair, as if to say, 'Well, here I am! Put that in your pipe and smoke it, Doctor.'

Aidan walked in as he must have walked everywhere he went. Softly, as I say, but certainly too. No social threshold to daunt him. No new relationship to embarrass his sense of self. He did not wait for my introduction but offered a hand and a level-eyed hello. He gave me the gentle cadence of his name. If I had received this greeting anywhere else, if I had been so politely wrong-footed in any other place, I might have felt a romantic stir.

I must have registered this alternative possibility in my mind for I felt a brief internal heat, a breath-lifting churn which made me want to look away from this man until I could collect myself. I looked down, seeking another place for my gaze to rest, to find some anodyne words written by a GP. What I saw instead was a trebling of the young man's image whose composure had so discomposed me, a triptych of him, an Aidan triumvirate. So, I flipped over the cardboard to find the GP letter with some urgency.

'Dear colleague,' it read, 'Please will you see this young man who has been unhappy with the shape of his nose for a long time. He would like to be considered for a rhinoplasty. I am arranging for photos to be taken.' No other details were given.

The morning, which until this patient had flowed smoothly, now went awry. I forgot the order of things. I didn't start at the beginning. Even though all I was attempting was a specific rhinology consultation, the history I took was too short, and nearly missed out several important points. I had to jam these things in at the last minute: any nasal blockage, history of trauma, previous surgery? The questions and the answers were all heaped up. And the whole nervy consultation ended with my asking, 'What is it you would like us to change?'

For this enquiry, I had moved my patient into the blue upholstered dentist's chair that was bolted to the floor in the middle of the room. The back of this chair urged Aidan to relax, it expected his back. Had he lain in it, he would have been in the perfect position for the ENT examination, made slightly passive. But though he sat in the chair, he did not permit its embrace. His feet were firmly planted on the footrest and his knees supported his hands. His fingers were chapped around the knuckles and the nailbeds were very long, and curved like sugared almonds.

He looked at me directly. What stopped him from being daunting in this constant alertness was the almost lisping softness of his voice, although its tone was pleasing and didn't make me itchy the way sibilant voices do. He moved now to his brief. And when he started, the vigour of his words surprised me.

'It's not how I'm meant to be. I really want it changed. It's ugly. Can you get rid of this bump here?'

With one long finger, he poked the bridge of his nose quite roughly, so that he blinked despite himself. Then he looked suddenly tired. He lifted his hands from his parted knees which he made into a lap to let his hands drop back on. He leaned his head back against the rest. The soft spikes of his hair fell backwards to show his ears, which were a funny shape, as the ears of good-looking people often are. I reached out my hand to just above his nose.

I said, 'The thing is, you have quite a small nose already. If we remove this hump, the danger is that your nose will look too feminine. It will look like a girl's nose.'

Aidan's body stayed as it was but the words he said next made it seem as if he had sat bolt upright. 'I want a girl's nose. I am a girl. I want to be a girl.' Exactly then the door burst open and my rambunctious boss came in. He probably thought that I was alone. My back was to the door, and my hand was still suspended in the air, above that organ which I now realised was hardly relevant. I must have looked shocked. Because when I swung around, surprised by my boss's entry, he went straight from 'Sorry' at having interrupted to 'What?' He forgot himself as a doctor. He had obviously sensed something was afoot.

I looked from one man to the other. Then, with my

eyes on Aidan, gauging his face, I said, 'This is one of the consultants, Mr Patel.' Then, taking several seconds to gather my thoughts, I addressed my consultant. 'This is Aidan. He has come in today to discuss the possibility of rhinoplasty. But I think he's just told me that he actually wants to be considered for gender reassignment.'

Mr Patel's shoulders, all hunched up with his usual restiveness, with the action of having just burst in, settled to the horizontal. 'Well. Gosh!' he said. 'I must say that's something I haven't come across before. You'd better come with me, young man. Let's sit down in my room and see what we should do next.'

He held his hand out to Aidan, who did not take it. But my patient looked at Mr Patel as he rose, keeping contact with the help he was being offered, as if wanting to keep alive this first breathing of the crisis he had not spoken of before, and had perhaps not even formulated until now.

Aidan went directly from Mr Patel's room back to his own GP that morning to embark on the process of having a sex change. That was the last time I saw him, but I did not forget how his true desire had manifested itself as something else, how one thing had come under the aegis of another. And I remembered him in the ensuing months, as I began to wonder whether there wasn't an unacknowledged undercurrent in my own life too.

The first conscious doubt I ever had about my commitment to surgery as a career occurred at an international ENT conference. It was less than a year after the morning that Aidan had walked into my consultation room. I was five months pregnant, and had been finding work tiring for the first time in my life. Standing up in theatre made me feel faint. When I got home in the evening, I couldn't find the energy to read up on the next day's surgery, because all I wanted to do was sleep. Getting out of bed in the middle of the night when on call had become a real challenge. I had been ascribing all this to the physiological glitch of pregnancy, and hoped only that I would soon be myself again.

So when I was invited to present some research at a prestigious meeting in Barcelona, I was grateful. I was determined to make the most of the opportunity and thought a successful performance would be just the boost I needed, exactly the right opportunity to re-engage with my surgery, and to refresh my love of my career.

The day before the conference, I travelled to Spain with some ENT colleagues. I spent the evening going through my presentation and, rising early the next morning, was the first to arrive at the conference centre. I checked on one of the noticeboards which room I was due to speak in. It turned out I was in the largest lecture theatre in the building, with a capacity of five hundred. My talk was scheduled for ten a.m., one of the first in the meeting.

I moseyed around the soulless building for hours, and gradually the conference centre filled up. There were clusters of Mediterranean surgeons all smoking, and English guys guffawed in groups. Eventually, I went into the lecture theatre and set up my computer. I projected the first slide of my PowerPoint presentation onto the screen in readiness. The stage I was standing on might have hosted the entire chorus of a Greek tragedy. I waited.

At five to ten, my boss turned up with another ENT colleague. The appointed hour came and went. 'European time,' one of the guys shouted up at me lamely, and the other one laughed. I shifted my weight from one foot to the other, and experimented with scraping one of my high heels across the parquet surface of the stage. Was it slippery? Was I in danger of sliding over when I clip-clopped off to the applause of the as yet invisible audience?

At five minutes past ten, I delivered my speech to the two surgeons who had heard it umpteen times already. The swing doors at the back of the lecture theatre bumped open once during this time to reveal a distant figure who obviously thought the better of his impulse and backed straight out again. There were no questions. Four hands clapped gigantically when I had finished. And that was it.

I felt pretty downcast after this. I had worked really hard for nothing, and I felt foolish. But what was odd was that I still felt miserable the next day, and indeed for the remainder of the conference. At one point on the journey home, while my colleagues were commiserating with me about my little defeat, I remember having a most surprising thought, which was 'No, I don't think I'm sad about having no audience for my presentation. And I don't think it's pregnancy either. There's something bigger going on. I think this is the tip of some iceberg.' When I look back now, that thought was the very beginning of a new start for me.

Doctors embarking on a career in surgery are choosing a clinical specialty earlier than they used to. And the further one progresses, the narrower this remit becomes. Such a system has the great benefit of ensuring an expert for any disease a patient might have. But there are risks too. Focusing on only one area may lead us as doctors to become blinkered to everything else. We may fail to identify problems simply because they fall outside our ken. And we may miss important changes which are occurring even closer to home.

HOME

When I started out in medicine, home was just a poky hospital room. As new doctors, we were provided with living quarters and informed that there would be little opportunity to leave work during our first apprenticeship year. The corridor along which these rooms were packed seemed to stretch to infinity like a textbook lesson in perspective. The sense of pride I felt, as I walked through the door that bore my doctor-prefixed surname for the first time, far outshone the character of the dwelling on the other side of it.

A replica of all the others, my cubby was small and square. There was a narrow bed and a desk screwed to the wall, whose work surface was hardly big enough to hold a book. There was a school-style chair, a cupboard and a basin. The patch of carpet underfoot was that pressed, felty type that has domesticated the floors of all the main institutions in my life.

Next to the bed was a dirty window which gave onto a ledge spattered with pigeon shit and a greasy skyline beyond. Standing there, I grew used to the sight of cigarette-mouthed colleagues, leaning out from their own rooms, at all hours of the day and night. I breathed in the foul air and felt like a holidaymaker on the cruise of a lifetime. I was on top of the world.

Though tiny, my home seemed a place of infinite space. The first time I sat alone in it, I summoned to mind images of virtuous solitariness from every Victorian novel I have ever read. And then mixed these governess-type notions with more intrepid ideas of soldier, pirate and explorer to come up with a heroic hybrid I projected as my future. This room of my own would be big enough to rest me after all manner of adventures, and I linked its plainness with the promise of my surgical life to be. I did nothing to personalise my room's hard walls or to make it more cosy. I loved its cold character in which I felt I flourished regardless. The only gesture I made was to install a small fridge, but this was welcomed by such a population of cockroaches that I soon got rid of it again.

Once I started doctoring, my room became a harbour. The first weeks of immersion in hospital medicine were the most packed of my life. Witnessing patients recover from sickness or surgery was a satisfying business of close incremental observation, like watching cress seeds sprout on blotting paper as a child. Equally interesting was seeing people whom medicine could not help. These cases of clinical degeneration showed me the minute by minute pathogenesis of diseases that had previously only been textbook truths. And as I paused in my room during odd moments of quiet to assimilate what I was learning, I felt

a sense of expansion which seemed to extend to everything. It was as if I, and the very walls around me, grew.

Until very recently, this room was my favourite ever
home, the space in which I remember feeling most myself.
So I was sad at the end of my first year in hospital medicine when I had to give it up to a more junior doctor
and find a place of my own. I didn't spend much time
in this new flat because I was usually at work. And when
I did go home I felt a bit ashamed of how bare it was.
What had been normal in my hospital home now just
seemed sad.

Later still, I married and had a child and so inherited
the kind of home I had half dreamed of in my girlhood.
But even then, my domestic situation presented problems.
The more time I spent away from work, the more it felt
as if my attachment to surgery was loosening. I resented
this, clinging ever more desperately to the hospital as the
landscape in which I intended to define myself. And I
welcomed the advice of a senior female surgical colleague
who encouraged me to 'Find a good nanny. Let the nanny
bond with the children. You get on with your surgery.'

I arranged things this way. I thought I was doing the
right thing by keeping my doubts in check. But then I met
Thomas. He was ten days old the first time I saw him.
By the time our ward round had reached the neonatal
ITU, we had already stopped at the beds of thirty-odd
other patients on countless other wards. His name was
just one among the others that remained on the A4 list I
held in my hand, in the same size font as all the adults,
despite his tininess. This piece of paper also told me he
was in hospital because of laryngomalacia, a benign condition that occurs in babies, where the voice box is softer

than it should be. The infant presents to medical attention in the first few weeks of life with a type of noisy breathing known as stridor. The symptom may be alarming to the parents but usually corrects itself. Thomas had been admitted that day, and was expected to be discharged within the next twenty-four hours. Our visit to the ITU would probably be routine, and I was glad of this because I was already late for clinic.

We approached the baby's place in the ITU. This was composed of his cot and a pulpit-like stand on which the notes and charts were set at a forty-five-degree angle. Around the cot were stands and machines, like alternative parents leaning in. And within this tableau was a mite of a baby in noticeably interesting clothes, to make up for the other areas in which life had not yet allowed him to be interesting because he was stuck here. A teddy with shiny fur almost crowded him out, a silly stand-in for the mother and father who had no hope themselves of fitting within the ice-cream-carton bed to lie alongside their infant and offer love.

The baby was sleeping. His parents weren't there. A nurse was sitting out her personal vigil next to Thomas's station. She nodded to the consultant and spoke with the peculiar over-familiar language that nurses use with the babies they care for. First she said a practical bit, 'Doing well', then a matey bit, 'He's a little champion', and then another practical bit, 'Should be off home tomorrow.'

We hardly stopped. We just looped behind the consultant like a bridal entourage might do if the aisle the bride was walking down happened to have a corner in it, or if that bride needed to do a U-turn to go back out whence she came.

But this short visit had been just long enough for me to feel a most unfamiliar feeling. As I had trailed past the plastic bed, I had looked in on this little boy absently. I had seen babies like him before and usually felt untouched by them, they seemed so strangely uninhabited by themselves. But this boy was so tight and small. So compactly, completely sleeping that I had felt something deepen, as if a single thin note in me had warmed into a major chord. I had wanted to approximate the baby somehow. I had wanted to touch his pebbled fist. I had experienced that sharp parental crave for nearness with a child, which does not let up with any amount of clasping and kissing and smelling.

I was surprised to feel this, and not just because it was a cold hospital day. And not just because this child was a stranger to me. The truth was that I had been doing a good job of relegating my maternal feelings to the five minutes I spent in my child's dim room after getting home from work each evening. I had allowed myself a more expansive kind of softness during the few months of my maternity leave. But I had chased out these feelings on my return to work, preferring the more familiar pleasures of stress and happy ambition. This ill and floodlit baby had called from me something my own child not managed in months.

We were now walking off the ITU. We were walking away from a hardly known infant whose intense sweetness had stupefied me. I felt sad that I would never see Thomas again.

It happened that I was on call that night, not just to my own hospital but to three others in the region. My home lay equidistant from all four places I might have to visit, so after checking with my juniors that no job seemed imminent, I collected my bag and went out to the hospital car park. This asphalt space was mainly dark now, though there was enough light to show all the darkly different shades of car, within which I found my own. I thought again of the obscure nursery in my house, where I would soon tread quietly to see my own little one sleeping soundly.

I had an image of myself as a dot on a map between two babies, one I was leaving, one I was heading towards. I pressed the pad on my car keys and heard-saw the beep-flash of the car unlocking itself. And then came another familiar electronic sound which was my pager, snug against my middle, calling me from somewhere. I let myself into my car, rang the switchboard and waited in the front seat while the woman there put me through to what turned out to be the neonatatal ITU. It did not surprise me that it was Thomas they were calling me about, although if it had turned out to be someone else, I would have forgotten that I felt this way.

The nurse I spoke to had a panty voice and said she was worried about him. She said his breathing had got worse in the last five minutes, that his oxygen saturations had dropped a little, and that he seemed to be struggling to get his breath. She didn't need to tell a coherent story. I didn't need to hear any more details. I was still junior enough an ENT registrar to have foremost in my fears the possibility of a really sick baby, a baby with an airway problem. And I was glad of the opportunity to see this boy again, to get back to him.

I reached the ITU in no time and knew where to find my charge. He was lying in his plastic bed as he had been earlier that day, but other things were different now.

Unimportantly, the sky through the hospital windows had darkened to invisible reflectiveness. Signally, the baby wasn't sleeping any more, he was crying. People now stood where drip stands had been earlier. A nurse, a mother, a father. Faces all anxious, leaning in like kings to the manger. The nurse was holding a tiny oxygen mask in her hand, and gingerly she was attempting to cover the baby's mouth and nose with it. But he was twisting his face away so that her hand kept springing back before nagging forwards again to meet the same rejection. The baby was crying spasmodically and with every intake of breath you could hear the stridor, that most frightening sound to hear coming from a child's mouth. That sound of air fighting its way past the vocal cords. Through a space of less than four millimetres.

Without introduction, I walked in. I reached into the plastic cot, my action a rough analogue of the urge I had felt earlier in the day. This was no time for tenderness. Right now, I was just the doctor intent on self-preservation via the preservation of this child. I needed to get the situation right. In one move, I picked up the boy, and flipped him over to hand him into his mother's arms face down. Into a prone position which often relieves some of the respiratory difficulty of laryngomalacia. The boy's mother's eyes lifted to meet my doctor's eyes without the need for words, as if she was simply asking, 'Tell me what to do.' But all I needed to say was, 'That's it. Like that.' Because she was already doing it. Her son was lying across her arm. He had stopped crying almost instantly and though the inspiratory stridor was still audible, it was a soft sound now. The mother seemed as relieved as I was, she in her shoes, I in mine. She had started up a little bouncing motion, a little normal nursery activity, as if her body were saying to the child, feel this movement which is natural and domestic, which is not a movement of fright or alarm. From my doctor's side, I changed tack too. Almost leisurely now, I pulled the tiny paediatric mask from the oxygen tube, from which the oxygen still hissed at its highest setting. I turned the dial down on the canister to make the hissing stop but leave some flow, and I handed the free end of the tube to the mother and asked her to hold it near but not too near to her baby's face, wherever she thought it could comfortably be.

When our eyes met to give and receive these simple messages, this woman and I, she seemed to me all mother. I could not imagine her anywhere but here doing anything but this. She was like the evolved heroine in a Jane Austen novel who has learned to ease a crisis through, who has become a proper woman. I wondered, in the brief post-fear hiatus that the quietening baby allowed, what she saw looking at me. Did I seem all doctor? Would it be impossible to envisage me elsewhere than this makeshift hospital home, doing this clinical caring? Was this in fact all I could imagine for myself? Was this all I was?

The baby was calm now. His respiratory rate had fallen. The stridor was muted. The saturations had risen again. The clinical picture in front of me had become what it ought to be.

But I did not rush home. I stayed a while. To stand apart from the baby, but be with him by watching him in his mother's arms. To observe how open love could be. A kind of newness in which I wanted to dip. I tried to do this with a couple of little pats, an unnecessary rearrangement of the position of the oxygen tube. The mother allowed this, willingly indulging the segue of crisis into comfort, this precipitation of two women, who had been acting practically, into cluckiness. She the proud mother, me the admiring doctor. My own baby seemed a distant sort of witness, afar, across town, on the outside of what I was trying to reach to the inside of. It was not my baby I had interacted with, about whose welfare I had felt panic turn to relief and affection. I had felt this closeness with a stranger's baby, a strange baby. Nothing had called me home to my own. I do not remember what I felt in my own child's room that night. That is not what I remember.

This incident did not resolve a crisis as such. For me, there had been no conscious feminist tug of work versus children. I had never encountered chauvinism in the hospital or at home, forcing me to make imprisoned decisions about what mattered most. I had, however, been aware for a long time of a jangled feeling, a sense of a piece out of place needing to be shaken back in, to give the clear picture. Somehow, meeting Thomas enabled that to happen, and made me turn quite certainly in a new direction.

The following month, I resigned from my career in ENT surgery. Relinquishing my training position, with its promise of yet more exams, on-calls and research, I opted for an easier and smaller route. I took up a fixed surgical job, with no potential for progress but which would still allow me to do operations on a small-scale and part-time basis. I chose a life with more home in it.

Sometimes, when I look back on my dreams of becoming a consultant surgeon, I feel sad about the notional future

I have given up. And occasionally, I baulk at the essentially female nature of the rearrangements I have made. But, for the most part, this is not so. I see myself as I am now, sitting in an operating theatre in the hospital which has become my second home. There is music on the CD player. The room is staffed with women, and the atmosphere is one of companionship. I am performing a wedge excision of a skin cancer from someone's ear. My consultant and friend Miss P is opposite me, cutting a second cancer from the same patient's face. She is a far grander surgeon than I will ever be, but today at least we are working together equally and silently, speaking only to ask each other for scalpel, forceps or diathermy. And beyond these walls, my real home awaits me.

ACKNOWLEDGEMENTS

Thanks to Dan Franklin, Claire Paterson, Ander Cohen, John Weston and Lisa Pitkin. And, most of all, to Lara Agnew.